# THE ROSE
# TATTOO

## BY TENNESSEE WILLIAMS

PLATS

Eli Wallach as Alvaro Mangiacavallo and Maureen Stapleton as
Serafina delle Rose in the original Broadway production of *The Rose Tattoo*.
*(Photo courtesy of Eli Wallach.)*

# TENNESSEE WILLIAMS

# THE ROSE
# TATTOO

INTRODUCTION BY
JOHN PATRICK SHANLEY

A NEW DIRECTIONS BOOK

Manufactured in the United States of America
New Directions Books are printed on acid-free paper.
First published clothbound by New Directions in 1951
First published as New Directions Paperbook 1172 in 2010

*Library of Congress Cataloging-in-Publication Data*
Williams, Tennessee, 1911-1983.
     The rose tattoo / by Tennessee Williams ; introduction by John
Patrick Shanley ; Jack Barbera. — 1st American paperback ed.
       p. cm.
     Includes bibliographical references.
     ISBN 978-0-8112-1882-5 (alk. paper)
1. Widows—Drama. 2. Truck drivers—Drama. 3. Radio plays. I. Shanley, John Patrick. II.
Barbera, Jack, III. Title.
     PS3545.I5365R6 2010
     812'.54—dc22          2009038667

10 9 8 7 6 5

New Directions Books are published for James Laughlin
by New Directions Publishing Corporation
80 Eighth Avenue, New York, NY 10011

# CONTENTS

# INTRODUCTION

*The Rose Tattoo* is over the top. It is a lurid play, redolent of the smell of goats, the cries of ragged children and squawking birds. Its perimeters are defined by women, hairy-legged women, gossiping clownish women, whores, and witches. The scenic descriptions call for red and more red. The language is riddled with roses, rose oil, wallpaper with a rose motif, rose tattoos, and a daughter named Rosa. The play is set on the Gulf Coast, in a Sicilian community. You can feel, just out of view, the phases of the sea.

Entering the world Tennessee Williams conjures here is like stepping inside a woman's reproductive cycle. The body of the play opens with a kind of vast menstruation. Everything is red, painful, wildly moody, and steeped in the feminine. Serafina is bloated, plaintive in the extreme, untouchable. Nothing moves. Life is in stasis. She is carrying a child she will not bring to term, waiting for a husband who will never come. But she is blind to her situation.

She is blind because of pride. She is in the grip of a classic hubris. Her marriage is ideal. Her husband is handsome and faithful. Her sex life is the best. She is with child. She has no need of charms or luck. It doesn't take a genius to see where this is going. Williams, it would seem, has his sights set on tragedy. Serafina is determined to hold on to her illusion of the perfected life even to the detriment of life itself.

Of course the gods turn on her. Her husband is murdered, she loses the baby, and she enters an abysmal swamp of narcissistic emotion. She wallows for three years, clutching her husband's ashes, refusing to progress beyond bathos to acceptance. Her life becomes a siege. She will not surrender her dream of perfection, though it is not aging well. Her pride, standing like a stone in a river, inefficiently holds back the flood of days. Life moves on around her, making her passion ridiculous.

Her daughter Rosa ripens into womanhood and falls in love with a sailor. Serafina does what she can to stop it. She makes the suitor swear he will not make Rosa a woman. But it is really Serafina herself that Serafina is fighting. She is struggling against her own animal lust and the secret knowledge of her heart. Her husband was unfaithful. The rose tattoo that he wore he shared with another woman, Estelle.

Is it love that makes Serafina jealous when the gossip of her husband's infidelity reaches her? Would love care? Or is it a rage to control the truth? Either way, the man is dead. What does it matter? It matters because if her husband was only a man, then she is only a woman, human like everyone else. If she is only a woman, then she is subject to the same low carnality and amorality as her husband. Her rage is that of a bourgeois matron. When it becomes clear that what most upsets Serafina is loss of status, we begin to understand the territory. This is not tragedy, though Serafina would like it to be. It is melodrama and it is comedy.

Comedy finds its opportunity and makes its entrance to deflate pretension and false seriousness. We have been, as it were, inside the story Serafina has been writing. But at this point, the play cracks open and we are allowed to laugh. She is just another mortal fool in a world of fools.

Serafina has become a fleshy burlesque of a woman. She tries stuffing herself into a girdle, but the effort is increasingly hopeless. Her humanity is spilling out all over. She is like a Lucien Freud figure modeled in red clay. When a new man, Alvaro, enters her life to court her, we see him through her eyes. He has her husband's perfect body, but the jug-eared head of a clown. She has neglected the physical in favor of a dream. As a result, the physical runs rampant and grotesque. Her suitor appears to be a carnival version of her husband. Her own body, unheeded, half clothed and unkempt, sweats and pants unconsciously in the presence of a potential sexual partner. She is literally perverted. Alvaro is a mirror held up to her. His arrival announces she is ridiculous.

Serafina's passion makes her see the whole world only as an extension of her own feelings. Her daughter's happiness is unimportant to her. She misses Rosa's high school graduation. She shows no interest that the girl was given an academic prize. She neglects to give her the wristwatch purchased for the occasion. The daughter only exists to justify the mother's battle against change. The withholding of the wristwatch is not mere oversight. Serafina wishes to hold back the clock because in the fullness of time her mortal flesh will force her to reenter life. The mother wants to remain ignorant of the truth so the daughter's education is a detriment. The mother wants to have sex so the daughter must not.

In this play, what fascinates is the way the material world shouts out its metaphors. Everything is symbolic to an absurd degree because the main character neglects the literal. She is living a dream and reality cries out to be heard. Only when she awakes, embracing at last a real lover and her own animal essence, does the world cease to be a gaudy jungle. It is then that she becomes credible. This is the journey of *The Rose Tattoo*.

There is no one else like Tennessee Williams. He cuts through time and space with a voice as gigantic as the night sky. He is afraid of nothing in human nature. Nothing repulses him but cruelty. He grabs up sex in both hands like an infant Hercules. Madness is always just around the corner. Comedy forces its rude way into locutions about love, about death, about motherhood, about spiritual longing. He created a language as big and restless as a thick river seeking the sea. Nothing can stop his work from reaching the human heart. My sixteen-year-old son Frank recently saw *Cat on a Hot Tin Roof*. It shook him with its love and hunger; it shook him and held him with its big hands. Tennessee Williams stands alone. I revere him. He's a giant.

John Patrick Shanley
October 2009

# THE ROSE
# TATTOO

*TO FRANK IN RETURN FOR SICILY*

# SCENES

## ACT ONE

## ACT TWO

## ACT THREE

*The Rose Tattoo* was first produced by Cheryl Crawford at the Erlanger Theater in Chicago on December 29, 1950. It had its Broadway opening on February 3, 1951, at the Martin Beck Theater in New York City, with Daniel Mann as director, setting by Boris Aronson and music by David Diamond. Production Associate: Bea Lawrence. Assistant to Producer: Paul Bigelow.

## Cast of the New York Production

| | |
|---|---|
| SALVATORE | Salvatore Mineo |
| VIVI | Judy Ratner |
| BRUNO | Salvatore Taormina |
| ASSUNTA | Ludmilla Toretzka |
| ROSA DELLE ROSE | Phyllis Love |
| SERAFINA DELLE ROSE | Maureen Stapleton |
| ESTELLE HOHENGARTEN | Sonia Sorel |
| THE STREGA | Daisy Belmore |
| GIUSEPPINA | Rossana San Marco |
| PEPPINA | Augusta Merighi |
| VIOLETTA | Vivian Nathan |
| MARIELLA | Penny Santon |
| TERESA | Nancy Franklin |
| FATHER DE LEO | Robert Carricart |
| A DOCTOR | Andrew Duggan |
| MISS YORKE | Dorrit Kelton |
| FLORA | Jane Hoffman |
| BESSIE | Florence Sundstrom |
| JACK HUNTER | Don Murray |
| THE SALESMAN | Eddie Hyans |
| ALVARO MANGIACAVALLO | Eli Wallach |
| A MAN | David Stewart |
| ANOTHER MAN | Martin Balsam |

# AUTHOR'S PRODUCTION NOTES

The locale of the play is a village populated mostly by Sicilians somewhere along the Gulf Coast between New Orleans and Mobile. The time is the present.

As the curtain rises we hear a Sicilian folk singer with a guitar. He is singing. At each major division of the play this song is resumed and it is completed at the final curtain.

The first lighting is extremely romantic. We see a frame cottage, in a rather poor state of repair, with a palm tree leaning dreamily over one end of it and a flimsy little entrance porch, with spindling pillars, sagging steps and broken rails, at the other end. The setting seems almost tropical, for, in addition to the palm trees, there are tall canes with feathery fronds and a fairly thick growth of pampas grass. These are growing on the slope of an embankment along which runs a highway, which is not visible, but the cars passing on it can occasionally be heard. The house has a rear door which cannot be seen. The facing wall of the cottage is either a transparency that lifts for the interior scenes, or is cut away to reveal the interior.

The romantic first lighting is that of late dusk, the sky a delicate blue with an opalescent shimmer more like water than air. Delicate points of light appear and disappear like lights reflected in a twilight harbor. The curtain rises well above the low tin roof of the cottage.

We see an interior that is as colorful as a booth at a carnival. There are many religious articles and pictures of ruby and gilt, the brass cage of a gaudy parrot, a large bowl of goldfish, cut-glass decanters and vases, rose-patterned wallpaper and a rose-colored carpet; everything is exclamatory in its brightness like the projection of a woman's heart passionately in love. There is a small shrine against the wall between the rooms, consisting of a prie-

4

*dieu and a little statue of the Madonna in a starry blue robe and gold crown. Before this burns always a vigil light in its ruby glass cup. Our purpose is to show these gaudy, childlike mysteries with sentiment and humor in equal measure, without ridicule and with respect for the religious yearnings they symbolize.*

*An outdoor sign indicates that Serafina, whose home the cottage is, does "SEWING." The interior furnishings give evidence of this vocation. The most salient feature is a collection of dressmaker's dummies. There are at least seven of these life-size mannequins, in various shapes and attitudes. [They will have to be made especially for the play as their purpose is not realistic. They have pliable joints so that their positions can be changed. Their arms terminate at the wrist. In all their attitudes there is an air of drama, somewhat like the poses of declamatory actresses of the old school.] Principal among them are a widow and a bride who face each other in violent attitudes, as though having a shrill argument, in the parlor. The widow's costume is complete from black-veiled hat to black slippers. The bride's featureless head wears a chaplet of orange blossoms from which is depended a flowing veil of white marquisette, and her net gown is trimmed in white satin—lustrous, immaculate.*

*Most of the dummies and sewing equipment are confined to the dining room which is also Serafina's work room. In that room there is a tall cupboard on top of which are several dusty bottles of imported Sicilian spumanti.*

*O slinger! crack the nut of my eye! my heart twittered with joy under the splendour of the quicklime, the bird sings O Senectus! ... the streams are in their beds like the cries of women and this world has more beauty than a ram's skin painted red!*

Saint-John Perse: *Anabasis*
T. S. ELIOT TRANSLATION

# ACT ONE

*It is the hour that the Italians call "prima sera," the beginning of dusk. Between the house and the palm tree burns the female star with an almost emerald luster.*

*The mothers of the neighborhood are beginning to call their children home to supper, in voices near and distant, urgent and tender, like the variable notes of wind and water. There are three children: Bruno, Salvatore, and Vivi, ranged in front of the house, one with a red paper kite, one with a hoop, and the little girl with a doll dressed as a clown. They are in attitudes of momentary repose, all looking up at something—a bird or a plane passing over—as the mothers' voices call them.*

BRUNO: The white flags are flying at the Coast Guard station.

SALVATORE: That means fair weather.

VIVI: I love fair weather.

GIUSEPPINA: Vivi! Vieni mangiare!

PEPPINA: Salvatore! Come home!

VIOLETTA: Bruno! Come home to supper!

[*The calls are repeated tenderly, musically.*

*The interior of the house begins to be visible. Serafina delle Rose is seen on the parlor sofa, waiting for her husband Rosario's return. Between the curtains is a table set lovingly for supper; there is wine in a silver ice-bucket and a great bowl of roses.*

*Serafina looks like a plump little Italian opera singer in the role of Madame Butterfly. Her black hair is done in a high pompadour that glitters like wet coal. A rose is held in place by glittering jet hairpins. Her voluptuous figure is sheathed in pale rose silk. On her feet are dainty slippers with glittering buckles and French heels. It is apparent from the way she sits, with such plump dignity, that she is wearing a tight girdle. She sits very erect, in an attitude of forced composure, her ankles daintily crossed and her plump little hands holding a yellow paper fan on which is painted a rose. Jewels gleam on her fingers, her wrists and her ears and about her throat. Expectancy shines in her eyes. For a few moments she seems to be posing for a picture.*

*Rosa delle Rose appears at the side of the house, near the palm tree. Rosa, the daughter of the house, is a young girl of twelve. She is pretty and vivacious, and has about her a particular intensity in every gesture.*]

SERAFINA: Rosa, where are you?

ROSA: Here, Mama.

SERAFINA: What are you doing, cara?

ROSA: I've caught twelve lightning bugs.

[*The cracked voice of Assunta is heard, approaching.*]

SERAFINA: I hear Assunta! Assunta!

[*Assunta appears and goes into the house, Rosa following her in. Assunta is an old woman in a gray shawl, bearing a basket of herbs, for she is a fattuchiere, a woman who practices a simple sort of medicine. As she enters the children scatter.*]

ASSUNTA: Vengo, vengo. Buona sera. Buona sera. There is something wild in the air, no wind but everything's moving.

SERAFINA: I don't see nothing moving and neither do you.

ASSUNTA: Nothing is moving so you can see it moving, but

everything is moving, and I can hear the star-noises. Hear them? Hear the star-noises?

SERAFINA: Naw, them ain't the star-noises. They're termites, eating the house up. What are you peddling, old woman, in those little white bags?

ASSUNTA: Powder, wonderful powder. You drop a pinch of it in your husband's coffee.

SERAFINA: What is it good for?

ASSUNTA: What is a husband good for! I make it out of the dry blood of a goat.

SERAFINA: Davero!

ASSUNTA: Wonderful stuff! But be sure you put it in his coffee at supper, not in his breakfast coffee.

SERAFINA: My husband don't need no powder!

ASSUNTA: Excuse me, Baronessa. Maybe he needs the opposite kind of a powder, I got that, too.

SERAFINA: Naw, naw, *no* kind of powder at all, old woman. [*She lifts her head with a proud smile.*]

[*Outside the sound of a truck is heard approaching up on the highway.*]

ROSA [*joyfully*]: Papa's truck!

[*They stand listening for a moment, but the truck goes by without stopping.*]

SERAFINA [*to Assunta*]: That wasn't him. It wasn't no 10-ton truck. It didn't rattle the shutters! Assunta, Assunta, undo a couple of hooks, the dress is tight on me!

9

ASSUNTA: Is it true what I told you?

SERAFINA: Yes, it is true, but nobody needed to tell me. Assunta, I'll tell you something which maybe you won't believe.

ASSUNTA: It is impossible to tell me anything that I don't believe.

SERAFINA: Va bene! Senti, Assunta!—I knew that I had conceived on the very night of conception! [*There is a phrase of music as she says this.*]

ASSUNTA: Ahhhh?

SERAFINA: Senti! That night I woke up with a burning pain on me, here, on my left breast! A pain like a needle, quick, quick, hot little stitches. I turned on the light, I uncovered my breast!—On it I saw the rose tattoo of my husband!

ASSUNTA: Rosario's tattoo?

SERAFINA: On me, on my breast, his tattoo! And when I saw it I knew that I had conceived . . .

[*Serafina throws her head back, smiling proudly, and opens her paper fan. Assunta stares at her gravely, then rises and hands her basket to Serafina.*]

ASSUNTA: Ecco! *You* sell the powders! [*She starts toward the door.*]

SERAFINA: You don't believe that I saw it?

ASSUNTA [*stopping*]: Did Rosario see it?

SERAFINA: I screamed. But when he woke up, it was gone. It only lasted a moment. But I *did* see it, and I *did* know, when I seen it, that I had conceived, that in my body another rose was growing!

ASSUNTA: Did he believe that you saw it?

SERAFINA: No. He laughed.—He laughed and I cried . . .

ASSUNTA: And he took you into his arms, and you stopped crying!

SERAFINA: Si!

ASSUNTA: Serafina, for you everything has got to be different. A sign, a miracle, a wonder of some kind. You speak to Our Lady. You say that She answers your questions. She nods or shakes Her head at you. Look, Serafina, underneath Our Lady you have a candle. The wind through the shutters makes the candle flicker. The shadows move. Our Lady seems to be nodding!

SERAFINA: She gives me signs.

ASSUNTA: Only to you? Because you are more important? The wife of a barone? Serafina! In Sicily they called his uncle a baron, but in Sicily everybody's a baron that owns a piece of the land and a separate house for the goats!

SERAFINA: They said to his uncle "Voscenza!" and they kissed their hands to him! [*She kisses the back of her hand repeatedly, with vehemence.*]

ASSUNTA: His uncle in Sicily!—Si—But *here* what's he do? Drives a truck of bananas?

SERAFINA [*blurting out*]: No! *Not* bananas!

ASSUNTA: Not bananas?

SERAFINA: Stai zitta! [*She makes a warning gesture.*]—No— Vieni qui, Assunta! [*She beckons her mysteriously. Assunta approaches.*]

ASSUNTA: Cosa dici?

11

SERAFINA: On top of the truck is bananas! But underneath—something else!

ASSUNTA: Che altre cose?

SERAFINA: Whatever it is that the Brothers Romano want hauled out of the state, he hauls it for them, underneath the bananas! [*She nods her head importantly.*] And money, he gets so much it spills from his pockets! Soon I don't have to make dresses!

ASSUNTA [*turning away*]: Soon I think you will have to make a black veil!

SERAFINA: Tonight is the last time he does it! Tomorrow he quits hauling stuff for the Brothers Romano! He pays for the 10-ton truck and works for himself. We live with dignity in America, then! Own truck! Own house! And in the house will be everything electric! Stove—deep-freeze—*tutto!*—But tonight, stay with me ... I can't swallow my heart!—Not till I hear the truck stop in front of the house and his key in the lock of the door!—When I call him, and him shouting back, *"Si, sono qui!"* In his hair, Assunta, he has—oil of roses. And when I wake up at night—the air, the dark room's—full of—roses ... Each time is the first time with him. Time doesn't pass ...

[*Assunta picks up a small clock on the cupboard and holds it to her ear.*]

ASSUNTA: Tick, tick, tick, tick. —You say the clock is a liar.

SERAFINA: No, the clock is a fool. I don't listen to it. My clock is my heart and my heart don't say tick-tick, it says love-love! And now I have two hearts in me, both of them saying love-love!

[*A truck is heard approaching, then passes. Serafina drops her fan. Assunta opens a bottle of spumanti with a loud pop. Serafina cries out.*]

ASSUNTA: Stai tranquilla! Calmati! [*She pours her a glass of wine.*] Drink this wine and before the glass is empty he'll be in your arms!

SERAFINA: I can't—swallow my heart!

ASSUNTA: A woman must not have a heart that is too big to swallow! [*She crosses to the door.*]

SERAFINA: Stay with me!

ASSUNTA: I have to visit a woman who drank rat poison because of a heart too big for her to swallow.

[*Assunta leaves. Serafina returns indolently to the sofa. She lifts her hands to her great swelling breasts and murmurs aloud:*]

SERAFINA: Oh, it's so wonderful, having *two* lives in the body, not *one* but two! [*Her hands slide down to her belly, luxuriously.*] I am heavy with life, I am big, big, big with life! [*She picks up a bowl of roses and goes into the back room.*]

[*Estelle Hohengarten appears in front of the house. She is a thin blonde woman in a dress of Egyptian design, and her blonde hair has an unnatural gloss in the clear, greenish dusk. Rosa appears from behind the house, calling out:*]

ROSA: Twenty lightning bugs, Mama!

ESTELLE: Little girl? Little girl?

ROSA [*resentfully*]: Are you talking to me? [*There is a pause.*]

ESTELLE: Come here. [*She looks Rosa over curiously.*] You're a twig off the old rosebush.—Is the lady that does the sewing in the house?

ROSA: Mama's at home.

ESTELLE: I'd like to see her.

ROSA: Mama?

SERAFINA: Dimi?

ROSA: There's a lady to see you.

SERAFINA: Oh. Tell her to wait in the parlor. [*Estelle enters and stares curiously about. She picks up a small framed picture on the cupboard. She is looking at it as Serafina enters with a bowl of roses. Serafina speaks sharply.*] That is my husband's picture.

ESTELLE: Oh!—I thought it was Valentino.—With a mustache.

SERAFINA [*putting the bowl down on the table*]: You want something?

ESTELLE: Yes. I heard you do sewing.

SERAFINA: Yes, I do sewing.

ESTELLE: How fast can you make a shirt for me?

SERAFINA: That all depends. [*She takes the picture from Estelle and puts it back on the cupboard.*]

ESTELLE: I got the piece of silk with me. I want it made into a shirt for a man I'm in love with. Tomorrow's the anniversary of the day we met... [*She unwraps a piece of rose-colored silk which she holds up like a banner.*]

SERAFINA [*involuntarily*]: Che bella stoffa!—Oh, that would be wonderful stuff for a lady's blouse or for a pair of pyjamas!

ESTELLE: I want a man's shirt made with it.

SERAFINA: Silk this color for a shirt for a *man*?

ESTELLE: This man is wild like a Gypsy.

SERAFINA: A woman should not encourage a man to be wild.

ESTELLE: A man that's wild is hard for a woman to hold, huh? But if he was tame—would the woman want to hold him? Huh?

SERAFINA: I am a married woman in business. I don't know nothing about wild men and wild women and I don't have much time—so . . .

ESTELLE: I'll pay you twice what you ask me.

[*Outside there is the sound of the goat bleating and the jingle of its harness; then the crash of wood splintering.*]

ROSA [*suddenly appearing at the door*]: Mama, the black goat is loose! [*She runs down the steps and stands watching the goat. Serafina crosses to the door.*]

THE STREGA [*in the distance*]: Hyeh, Billy, hyeh, hyeh, Billy!

ESTELLE: I'll pay you three times the price that you ask me for it.

SERAFINA [*shouting*]: Watch the goat! Don't let him get in our yard! [*To Estelle.*]—If I ask you five dollars?

ESTELLE: I will pay you fifteen. Make it twenty; money is not the object. But it's got to be ready tomorrow.

SERAFINA: Tomorrow?

ESTELLE: Twenty-five dollars! [*Serafina nods slowly with a stunned look. Estelle smiles.*] I've got the measurements with me.

SERAFINA: Pin the measurements and your name on the silk and the shirt will be ready tomorrow.

ESTELLE: My name is Estelle Hohengarten.

[*A little boy races excitedly into the yard.*]

THE BOY: Rosa, Rosa, the black goat's in your yard!

ROSA [*calling*]: Mama, the goat's in the yard!

SERAFINA [*furiously, forgetting her visitor*]: Il becco della strega!—Scusi! [*She runs out onto the porch.*] Catch him, catch him before he gets at the vines!

[*Rosa dances gleefully. The Strega runs into the yard. She has a mop of wild grey hair and is holding her black shirts up from her bare hairy legs. The sound of the goat's bleating and the jingling of his harness is heard in the windy blue dusk.*

*Serafina descends the porch steps. The high-heeled slippers, the tight silk skirt and the dignity of a baronessa make the descent a little gingerly. Arrived in the yard, she directs the goat-chase imperiously with her yellow paper fan, pointing this way and that, exclaiming in Italian.*

*She fans herself rapidly and crosses back of the house. The goat evidently makes a sudden charge. Screaming, Serafina rushes back to the front of the house, all out of breath, the glittering pompadour beginning to tumble down over her forehead.*]

SERAFINA: Rosa! You go in the house! Don't look at the Strega!

[*Alone in the parlor, Estelle takes the picture of Rosario. Impetuously, she thrusts it in her purse and runs from the house, just as Serafina returns to the front yard.*]

ROSA [*refusing to move*]: Why do you call her a witch?

[*Serafina seizes her daughter's arm and propels her into the house.*]

SERAFINA: She has white eyes and every finger is crooked. [*She pulls Rosa's arm.*]

ROSA: She has a cataract, Mama, and her fingers are crooked because she has rheumatism!

SERAFINA: Malocchio—the evil eye—*that's* what she's got! And her fingers are crooked because she shook hands with the Devil. Go in the house and wash your face with salt water and throw the salt water away! *Go in! Quick!* She's coming!

[*The boy utters a cry of triumph.*

*Serafina crosses abruptly to the porch. At the same moment the boy runs triumphantly around the house leading the captured goat by its bell harness. It is a middle-sized black goat with great yellow eyes. The Strega runs behind with the broken rope. As the grotesque little procession runs before her—the Strega, the goat and the children—Serafina cries out shrilly. She crouches over and covers her face. The Strega looks back at her with a derisive cackle.*]

SERAFINA: Malocchio! Malocchio!

[*Shielding her face with one hand, Serafina makes the sign of the horns with the other to ward off the evil eye. And the scene dims out.*]

*It is just before dawn the next day. Father De Leo, a priest, and several black-shawled women, including Assunta, are standing outside the house. The interior of the house is very dim.*

GIUSEPPINA: There is a light in the house.

PEPPINA: I hear the sewing machine!

VIOLETTA: There's Serafina! She's working. She's holding up a piece of rose-colored silk.

ASSUNTA: She hears our voices.

VIOLETTA: She's dropped the silk to the floor and she's . . .

GIUSEPPINA: Holding her throat! I think she . . .

PEPPINA: Who's going to tell her?

VIOLETTA: Father De Leo will tell her.

FATHER DE LEO: I think a woman should tell her. I think Assunta must tell her that Rosario is dead.

ASSUNTA: It will not be necessary to tell her. She will know when she sees us.

[*It grows lighter inside the house. Serafina is standing in a frozen attitude with her hand clutching her throat and her eyes staring fearfully toward the sound of voices.*]

ASSUNTA: I think she already knows what we have come to tell her!

FATHER DE LEO: Andiamo, Signore! We must go to the door.

[*They climb the porch steps. Assunta opens the door.*]

SERAFINA [*gasping*]: Don't speak!

[*She retreats from the group, stumbling blindly backward among the dressmaker's dummies. With a gasp she turns and runs out the backdoor. In a few moments we see her staggering about outside near the palm tree. She comes down in front of the house, and stares blindly off into the distance.*]

SERAFINA [*wildly*]: Don't speak!

[*The voices of the women begin keening in the house. Assunta comes out and approaches Serafina with her arms extended. Serafina slumps to her knees, whispering hoarsely: "Don't speak!" Assunta envelopes her in the gray shawl of pity as the scene dims out.*]

*It is noon of the same day. Assunta is removing a funeral wreath on the door of the house. A doctor and Father De Leo are on the porch.*

THE DOCTOR: She's lost the baby. [*Assunta utters a low moan of pity and crosses herself.*] Serafina's a very strong woman and that won't kill her. But she is trying not to breathe. She's got to be watched and not allowed out of the bed. [*He removes a hypodermic and a small package from his bag and hands them to Assunta.*] —This is morphia. In the arm with the needle if she screams or struggles to get up again.

ASSUNTA: Capisco!

FATHER DE LEO: One thing I want to make plain. The body of Rosario must not be burned.

THE DOCTOR: Have you seen the "body of Rosario?"

FATHER DE LEO: Yes, I have seen his body.

THE DOCTOR: Wouldn't you say it was burned?

FATHER DE LEO: Of course the body was burned. When he was shot at the wheel of the truck, it crashed and caught fire. But deliberate cremation is not the same thing. It's an abomination in the sight of God.

THE DOCTOR: Abominations are something I don't know about.

FATHER DE LEO: The Church has set down certain laws.

THE DOCTOR: But the instructions of a widow have to be carried out.

FATHER DE LEO: Don't you know why she wants the body cremated? So she can keep the ashes here in the house.

THE DOCTOR: Well, why not, if that's any comfort to her?

FATHER DE LEO: Pagan idolatry is what I call it!

THE DOCTOR: Father De Leo, you love your people but you don't understand them. They find God in each other. And when they lose each other, they lose God and they're lost. And it's hard to help them.—Who is that woman?

[*Estelle Hohengarten has appeared before the house. She is black-veiled, and bearing a bouquet of roses.*]

ESTELLE: I am Estelle Hohengarten.

[*Instantly there is a great hubbub in the house. The women mourners flock out to the porch, whispering and gesticulating excitedly.*]

FATHER DE LEO: What have you come here for?

ESTELLE: To say good-bye to the body.

FATHER DE LEO: The casket is closed; the body cannot be seen. And you must never come here. The widow knows nothing about you. Nothing at all.

GIUSEPPINA: *We* know about you!

PEPPINA: Va via! Sporcacciona!

VIOLETTA: Puttana!

MARIELLA: Assassina!

TERESA: You sent him to the Romanos.

FATHER DE LEO: Shhh!

[*Suddenly the women swarm down the steps like a cloud of attaching birds, all crying out in Sicilian. Estelle crouches and bows her head defensively before their savage assault. The bouquet of roses is snatched from her black-gloved hands and she*] *is flailed with them about the head and shoulders. The thorns catch her veil and tear it away from her head. She covers her white sobbing face with her hands.]*

FATHER DE LEO: Ferme! Ferme! Signore, fermate vi nel nome di Dio!—Have a little respect!

*[The women fall back from Estelle, who huddles weeping on the walk.]*

ESTELLE: See him, see him, just see him . . .

FATHER DE LEO: The body is crushed and burned. Nobody can see it. Now go away and don't ever come here again, Estelle Hohengarten!

THE WOMEN [*in both languages, wildly*]: Va via, va via, go away.

*[Rosa comes around the house. Estelle turns and retreats. One of the mourners spits and kicks at the tangled veil and roses. Father De Leo leaves. The others return inside, except Rosa.*

*After a few moments the child goes over to the roses. She picks them up and carefully untangles the veil from the thorns.*

*She sits on the sagging steps and puts the black veil over her head. Then for the first time she begins to weep, wildly, histrionically. The little boy appears and gazes at her; momentarily impressed by her performance. Then he picks up a rubber ball and begins to bounce it.*

*Rosa is outraged. She jumps up, tears off the veil and runs to the little boy, giving him a sound smack and snatching the ball away from him.]*

ROSA: Go home! My papa is dead!

*[The scene dims out, as the music is heard again.]*

*A June day, three years later. It is morning and the light is bright. A group of local mothers are storming Serafina's house, indignant over her delay in delivering the graduation dresses for their daughters. Most of the women are chattering continually in Sicilian, racing about the house and banging the doors and shutters. The scene moves swiftly and violently until the moment when Rosa finally comes out in her graduation dress.*

GIUSEPPINA: Serafina! Serafina delle Rose!

PEPPINA: Maybe if you call her "Baronessa" she will answer the door. [*With a mocking laugh.*] Call her "Baronessa" and kiss your hand to her when she opens the door.

GIUSEPPINA [*tauntingly*]: Baronessa! [*She kisses her hand toward the door.*]

VIOLETTA: When did she promise your dress?

PEPPINA: All week she say, "Domani—domani—domani." But yestiddy I told her . . .

VIOLETTA: Yeah?

PEPPINA: Oh yeah. I says to her, "Serafina, domani's the high school graduation. I got to try the dress on my daughter *today.*" "Domani," she says, "Sicuro! sicuro! sicuro!" So I start to go away. Then I hear a voice call, "Signora! Signora!" So I turn round and I see Serafina's daughter at the window.

VIOLETTA: Rosa?

PEPPINA: Yeah, Rosa. An' you know how?

VIOLETTA: How?

PEPPINA: *Naked!* Nuda, nuda! [*She crosses herself and repeats a prayer.*] In nominis padri et figlio et spiritus sancti. Aaahh!

VIOLETTA: What did she do?

PEPPINA: Do? She say, "Signora! Please, you call this numero and ask for Jack and tell Jack my clothes are lock up so I can't get out from the house." Then Serafina come and she grab-a the girl by the hair and she pull her way from the window and she slam the shutters right in my face!

GIUSEPPINA: Whatsa the matter the daughter?

VIOLETTA: Who is this boy? Where did she meet him?

PEPPINA: Boy! What boy? He's a sailor. [*At the word "sailor" the women say "Ahhh!"*] She met him at the high school dance and somebody tell Serafina. That's why she lock up the girl's clothes so she can't leave the house. She can't even go to the high school to take the examinations. Imagine!

VIOLETTA: Peppina, this time *you* go to the door, yeah?

PEPPINA: Oh yeah, I go. Now I'm getting nervous. [*The women all crowd to the door.*] Sera-feee-na!

VIOLETTA: Louder, louder!

PEPPINA: Apri la porta! Come on, come on!

THE WOMEN [*together*]: Yeah, apri la porta!... Come on, hurry up!... Open up!

GIUSEPPINA: I go get-a police.

VIOLETTA: Whatsa matta? You want more trouble?

GIUSEPPINA: Listen, I pay in advance five dollars and get no dress. Now what she wear, my daughter, to graduate in? A couple of towels and a rose in the hair? [*There is a noise inside: a shout and running footsteps.*]

THE WOMEN: Something is going on in the house! I hear someone! Don't I? Don't you?

[*A scream and running footsteps are heard. The front door
opens and Serafina staggers out onto the porch. She is wearing
a soiled pink slip and her hair is wild.*]

SERAFINA: Aiuto! Aiuto! [*She plunges back into the house.*]

[*Miss Yorke, a spinsterish high school teacher, walks quickly up
to the house. The Sicilian women, now all chattering at once
like a cloud of birds, sweep about her as she approaches.*]

MISS YORKE: You ladies know I don't understand Italian! So,
please . . .

[*She goes directly into the house. There are more outcries inside. The Strega comes and stands at the edge of the yard, cackling derisively.*]

THE STREGA [*calling back to someone*]: The Wops are at it
again!–She got the daughter lock up naked in there all week. Ho,
ho, ho! She lock up all week–naked–shouting out the window
tell people to call a number and give a message to Jack. Ho, ho,
ho! I guess she's in trouble already, and only fifteen!–They ain't
civilized, these Sicilians. In the old country they live in caves in the
hills and the country's run by bandits. Ho, ho, ho! More of them
coming over on the boats all the time. [*The door is thrown open
again and Serafina reappears on the porch. She is acting wildly, as
if demented.*]

SERAFINA [*gasping in a hoarse whisper*]: She cut her wrist, my
daughter, she cut her wrist! [*She runs out into the yard.*] Aiiii-eeee!
Aiutatemi, aiutatemi! Call the dottore! [*Assunta rushes up to Serafina and supports her as she is about to fall to her knees in the
yard.*] Get the knife away from her! Get the knife, please! Get the

knife away from—she cut her wrist with—Madonna! Madonna
mia . . .

ASSUNTA: Smettila, smettila, Serafina.

MISS YORKE [*coming out of the back room*]: Mrs. Delle Rose,
your daughter has not cut her wrist. Now come back into the
house.

SERAFINA [*panting*]: Che dice, che dice? Che cosa? Che cosa
dice?

MISS YORKE: Your daughter's all right. Come back into the
house. And you ladies please go away!

ASSUNTA: Vieni, Serafina. Andiamo a casa. [*She supports the
heavy, sagging bulk of Serafina to the steps. As they climb the steps
one of the Sicilian mothers advances from the whispering group.*]

GIUSEPPINA [*boldly*]: Serafina, we don't go away until we get
our dresses.

PEPPINA: The graduation begins and the girls ain't dressed.

[*Serafina's reply to this ill-timed request is a long, animal howl
of misery as she is supported into the house. Miss Yorke follows and firmly closes the door upon the women, who then go
around back of the house. The interior of the house is lighted
up.*]

MISS YORKE [*to Serafina*]: No, no, no, she's not bleeding. Rosa?
Rosa, come here and show your mother that you are not bleeding
to death.

[*Rosa appears silently and sullenly between the curtains that
separate the two rooms. She has a small white handkerchief
tied around one wrist. Serafina points at the wrist and cries out:
"Aiieee!"*]

MISS YORKE [*severely*]: Now *stop* that, Mrs. Delle Rose!

[*Serafina rushes to Rosa, who thrusts her roughly away.*]

ROSA: Lasciami stare, Mama! —I'm so ashamed I could die. This is the way she goes around all the time. She hasn't put on clothes since my father was killed. For three years she sits at the sewing machine and never puts a dress on or goes out of the house, and now she has locked my clothes up so *I* can't go out. She wants me to be like her, a freak of the neighborhood, the way she is! Next time, next time, I won't cut my wrist but my throat! I don't want to live locked up with a bottle of ashes! [*She points to the shrine.*]

ASSUNTA: Figlia, figlia, figlia, non devi parlare cosí!

MISS YORKE: Mrs. Delle Rose, please give me the key to the closet so that your daughter can dress for the graduation!

SERAFINA [*surrendering the key.*] Ecco la—chiave... [*Rosa snatches the key and runs back through the curtains.*]

MISS YORKE: Now why did you lock her clothes up, Mrs. Delle Rose?

SERAFINA: The wrist is still bleeding!

MISS YORKE: No, the wrist is not bleeding. It's just a skin cut, a scratch. But the child is exhausted from all this excitement and hasn't eaten a thing in two or three days.

ROSA [*running into the dining room*]: Four days! I only asked her one favor. Not to let me go out but to let Jack come to the house so she could meet him! —Then she locked my clothes up!

MISS YORKE: Your daughter missed her final examinations at the high school, but her grades have been so good that she will be allowed to graduate with her class and take the examinations later. —You understand me, Mrs. Delle Rose!

27

[*Rosa goes into the back of the house.*]

SERAFINA [*standing at the curtains*]: See the way she looks at me? I've got a wild thing in the house, and her wrist is still bleeding!

MISS YORKE: Let's not have any more outbursts of emotion!

SERAFINA: Outbursts of—you make me sick! Sick! Sick at my stomach you make me! Your school, you make all this trouble! You give-a this dance where she gets mixed up with a sailor.

MISS YORKE: You are talking about the Hunter girl's brother, a sailor named Jack, who attended the dance with his sister?

SERAFINA: "Attended with sister!"—Attended with *sister!*— My daughter, she's nobody's sister!

[*Rosa comes out of the back room. She is radiantly beautiful in her graduation gown.*]

ROSA: Don't listen to her, don't pay any attention to her, Miss Yorke.—I'm ready to go to the high school.

SERAFINA [*stunned by her daughter's beauty, and speaking with a wheedling tone and gestures, as she crouches a little*]: O tesoro, tesoro! Vieni qua, Rosa, cara!—Come here and kiss Mama one minute!—Don't go like that, now!

ROSA: Lasciami stare!

[*She rushes out on the porch. Serafina gazes after her with arms slowly drooping from their imploring gesture and jaw dropping open in a look of almost comic desolation.*]

SERAFINA: Ho solo te, solo te—in questo mondo!

MISS YORKE: Now, now, Mrs. Delle Rose, no more excitement, please!

SERAFINA [*suddenly plunging after them in a burst of fury*]: Senti, senti, per favore!

ROSA: Don't you dare come out on the street like that!—*Mama!*

[*She crouches and covers her face in shame, as Serafina heedlessly plunges out into the front yard in her shocking deshabille, making wild gestures.*]

SERAFINA: You give this dance where she gets mixed up with a sailor. What do you think you want to do at this high school? [*In weeping despair, Rosa runs to the porch.*] How high is this high school? Listen, how high is this high school? Look, look, look, I will show you! It's high as that horse's dirt out there in the street! [*Serafina points violently out in front of the house.*] Si! 'Sta fetentissima scuola! Scuola maledetta!

[*Rosa cries out and rushes over to the palm tree, leaning against it, with tears of mortification.*]

MISS YORKE: Mrs. Delle Rose, you are talking and behaving extremely badly. I don't understand how a woman that acts like you could have such a sweet and refined young girl for a daughter!—You don't deserve it!—Really... [*She crosses to the palm tree.*]

SERAFINA: Oh, you want me to talk refined to you, do you? Then do me one thing! Stop ruining the girls at the high school! [*As Serafina paces about, she swings her hips in the exaggeratedly belligerent style of a parading matador.*]

ASSUNTA: Piantala, Serafina! Andiamo a casa!

SERAFINA: No, no, I ain't through talking to this here teacher!

ASSUNTA: Serafina, look at yourself, you're not dressed!

SERAFINA: I'm dressed okay; I'm not naked! [*She glares savagely at the teacher by the palm tree. The Sicilian mothers return to the front yard.*]

ASSUNTA: Serafina, cara? Andiamo a casa, adesso!—Basta! Basta!

SERAFINA: Aspetta!

ROSA: I'm so ashamed I could die, I'm so ashamed. Oh, you don't know, Miss Yorke, the way that we live. She never puts on a dress; she stays all the time in that dirty old pink slip! —And talks to my father's ashes like he was living.

SERAFINA: Teacher! Teacher, senti! What do you think you want to do at this high school? Sentite! per favore! You give this a dance! What kind of a spring dance is it? Answer this question, please, for me! What kind of a spring dance is it? She meet this boy there who don't even go to no high school. What kind of a boy? Guardate! *A sailor that wears a gold earring!* That kind of a boy is the kind of boy she meets there! —That's why I lock her clothes up so she can't go back to the high school! [*Suddenly to Assunta.*] She cut her wrist! It's still bleeding! [*She strikes her forehead three times with her fist.*]

ROSA: Mama, you look disgusting! [*She rushes away.*]

[*Miss Yorke rushes after her. Serafina shades her eyes with one hand to watch them departing down the street in the brilliant spring light.*]

SERAFINA: Did you hear what my daughter said to me? —"You look—disgusting." —She calls me . . .

ASSUNTA: Now, Serafina, we must go in the house. [*She leads her gently to the porch of the little house.*]

SERAFINA [*proudly*]: How pretty she look, my daughter, in the white dress, like a bride! [*To all.*] Excuse me! Excuse me, please! Go away! Get out of my yard!

GIUSEPPINA [*taking the bull by the horns*]: No, we ain't going to go without the dresses!

ASSUNTA: Give the ladies the dresses so the girls can get dressed for the graduation.

SERAFINA: That one there, she only paid for the goods. I charge for the work.

GIUSEPPINA: Ecco! I got the money!

THE WOMEN: We *got* the money!

SERAFINA: The names are pinned on the dresses. Go in and get them. [*She turns to Assunta.*] Did you hear what my daughter called me? She called me "disgusting!"

[*Serafina enters the house, slamming the door. After a moment the mothers come out, cradling the white voile dresses tenderly in their arms, murmuring "carino!" and "bellissimo!"*
*As they disappear the inside light is brought up and we see Serafina standing before a glazed mirror, looking at herself and repeating the daughter's word.*]

SERAFINA: Disgusting!

[*The music is briefly resumed to mark a division.*]

*Immediately following. Serafina's movements gather momentum. She snatches a long-neglected girdle out of a bureau drawer and holds it experimentally about her waist. She shades her head doubtfully, drops the girdle and suddenly snatches the $8.98 hat off the millinery dummy and plants it on her head. She turns around distractedly, not remembering where the mirror is. She gasps with astonishment when she catches sight of herself, snatches the hat off and hastily restores it to the blank head of the dummy. She makes another confused revolution or two, then gasps with fresh inspiration and snatches a girlish frock off a dummy—an Alice-blue gown with daisies crocheted on it. The dress sticks on the dummy. Serafina mutters savagely in Sicilian. She finally overcomes this difficulty but in her exasperation she knocks the dummy over. She throws off the robe and steps hopefully into the gown. But she discovers it won't fit over her hips. She seizes the girdle again; then hurls it angrily away. The parrot calls to her; she yells angrily back at the parrot: "Zitto!"*

*In the distance the high school band starts playing. Serafina gets panicky that she will miss the graduation ceremonies, and hammers her forehead with her fist, sobbing a little. She wriggles despairingly out of the blue dress and runs out back in her rayon slip just as Flora and Bessie appear outside the house. Flora and Bessie are two female clowns of middle years and juvenile temperament. Flora is tall and angular; Bessie is rather stubby. They are dressed for a gala. Flora runs up the steps and bangs at the cottage door.*

BESSIE: I fail to understand why it's so important to pick up a polka-dot blouse when it's likely to make us miss the twelve o'clock train.

FLORA: Serafina! Serafina!

BESSIE: We only got fifteen minutes to get to the depot and I'll get faint on the train if I don't have m' coffee . . .

FLORA: Git a Coke on th' train, Bessie.

BESSIE: Git nothing on the train if we don't git the train!

[*Serafina runs back out of the bedroom, quite breathless, in a purple silk dress. As she passes the millinery dummy she snatches the hat off again and plants it back on her head.*]

SERAFINA: Wrist watch! Wrist watch! Where'd I put th' wrist watch? [*She hears Flora shouting and banging and rushes to the door.*]

BESSIE: Try the door if it ain't open.

FLORA [*pushing in*]: Just tell me, is it ready or not?

SERAFINA: Oh! You. Don't bother me. I'm late for the graduation of my daughter and now I can't find her graduation present.

FLORA: You got plenty of time.

SERAFINA: Don't you hear the band playing?

FLORA: They're just warming up. Now, Serafina, where is my blouse?

SERAFINA: Blouse? Not ready! I had to make fourteen graduation dresses!

FLORA: A promise is a promise and an excuse is just an excuse!

SERAFINA: I got to get to the high school!

FLORA: I got to get to the depot in that blouse!

BESSIE: We're going to the American Legion parade in New Orleans.

FLORA: There, there, there, there it is! [*She grabs the blouse from the machine.*] Get started, woman, stitch them bandanas together! If you don't do it, I'm a-gonna report you to the Chamber of Commerce and git your license revoked!

SERAFINA [*anxiously*]: What license you talking about? I got no license!

FLORA: You hear that, Bessie? *She hasn't got no license!*

BESSIE: *She ain't even got a license?*

SERAFINA [*crossing quickly to the machine*]: I—I'll stitch them together! But if you make me late to my daughter's graduation, I'll make you sorry some way . . .

[*She works with furious rapidity. A train whistle is heard.*]

BESSIE [*wildly and striking at Flora with her purse*]: Train's pullin' out! Oh, God, you made us miss it!

FLORA: Bessie, you know there's another at 12:45!

BESSIE: It's the selfish—principle of it that makes me sick! [*She walks rapidly up and down.*]

FLORA: Set down, Bessie. Don't wear out your feet before we git to th' city . . .

BESSIE: Molly tole me the town was full of excitement. They're dropping paper sacks full of water out of hotel windows.

FLORA: Which hotel are they dropping paper sacks out of?

BESSIE: What a fool question! The Monteleone Hotel.

FLORA: That's an old-fashioned hotel.

BESSIE: It might be old-fashioned but you'd be surprised at some of the modern, up-to-date things that go on there.

FLORA: I heard, I heard that the Legionnaires caught a girl on Canal Street! They tore the clothes off her and sent her home in a taxi!

BESSIE: I double dog dare anybody to try that on me!

FLORA: You?! Huh! You never need any assistance gittin' undressed!

SERAFINA [ominously]: You two ladies watch how you talk in there. This here is a Catholic house. You are sitting in the same room with Our Lady and with the blessed ashes of my husband!

FLORA [acidly]: Well, ex-cuse me! [She whispers maliciously to Bessie.] It sure is a pleasant surprise to see you wearing a dress, Serafina, but the surprise would be twice as pleasant if it was more the right size. [To Bessie, loudly.] She used to have a sweet figure, a little bit plump but attractive, but setting there at that sewing machine for three years in a kimona and not stepping out of the house has naturally given her hips!

SERAFINA: If I didn't have hips I would be a very uncomfortable woman when I set down.

[The parrot squawks. Serafina imitates its squawk.]

FLORA: Polly want a cracker?

SERAFINA: No. He don't want a cracker! What is she doing over there at that window?

BESSIE: Some Legionnaires are on the highway!

FLORA: A Legionnaire? No kidding?

[She springs up and joins her girl friend at the window. They both laugh fatuously, bobbing their heads out the window.]

BESSIE: He's looking this way; yell something!

FLORA [*leaning out the window*]: Mademoiselle from Armentieres, parley-voo!

BESSIE [*chiming in rapturously*]: Mademoiselle from Armentieres, parley-voo!

A VOICE OUTSIDE [*gallantly returning the salute*]: Mademoiselle from Armentieres, hadn't been kissed for forty years!

BOTH GIRLS [*together; very gaily*]: Hinky-dinky parley-voooo!

[*They laugh and applaud at the window. The Legionnaires are heard laughing. A car horn is heard as the Legionnaires drive away. Serafina springs up and rushes over to the window, jerks them away from it and slams the shutters in their faces.*]

SERAFINA [*furiously*]: I told you wimmen that you was not in a honky-tonk! Now take your blouse and git out! Get out on the streets where you kind a wimmen belong. —This is the house of Rosario delle Rose and those are his ashes in that marble urn and I won't have—unproper things going on here or dirty talk, neither!

FLORA: Who's talking dirty?

BESSIE: What a helluva nerve.

FLORA: I want you to listen!

SERAFINA: You are, you are, dirty talk, all the time men, men, men! You men-crazy things, you!

FLORA: Sour grapes—sour grapes is your trouble! You're wild with envy!

BESSIE: Isn't she green with jealousy? Huh!

SERAFINA [*suddenly and religiously*]: When I think of men I think about my husband. My husband was a Sicilian. We had love together every night of the week, we never skipped one, from the night we was married till the night he was killed in his fruit truck on that road there! [*She catches her breath in a sob.*] And maybe that is the reason I'm not man-crazy and don't like hearing the talk of women that are. But I am interested, now, in the happiness of my daughter who's graduating this morning out of high school. And now I'm going to be late, the band is playing! And I have lost her wrist watch!–her graduation present! [*She whirls about distractedly.*]

BESSIE: Flora, let's go!–The hell with that goddam blouse!

FLORA: Oh, no, just wait a minute! I don't accept insults from no one!

SERAFINA: Go on, go on to New Orleans, you two man-crazy things, you! And pick up a man on Canal Street but not in my house, at my window, in front of my dead husband's ashes! [*The high school band is playing a martial air in the distance. Serafina's chest is heaving violently; she touches her heart and momentarily seems to forget that she must go.*] I am not at all interested, I am not interested in men getting fat and bald in soldier-boy play suits, tearing the clothes off girls on Canal Street and dropping paper sacks out of hotel windows. I'm just not interested in that sort of man-crazy business. I remember my husband with a body like a young boy and hair on his head as thick and black as mine is and skin on him smooth and sweet as a yellow rose petal.

FLORA: Oh, a *rose*, was he?

SERAFINA: Yes, yes, a rose, a rose!

FLORA: Yes, a rose of a Wop!–of a gangster!–shot smuggling dope under a load of bananas!

BESSIE: Flora, Flora, let's go!

SERAFINA: My folks was peasants, contadini, but he–he come from *land*owners! *Signorile,* my husband–at night I sit here and

37

I'm satisfied to remember, because I had the best. —Not the third best and not the second best, but the *first* best, the *only* best! —So now I stay here and am satisfied now to remember. . . .

BESSIE: Come on, come out! To the depot!

FLORA: Just wait, I wanta hear this, it's too good to miss!

SERAFINA: I count up the nights I held him all night in my arms, and I can tell you how many. Each night for twelve years. Four thousand—three hundred—and eighty. The number of nights I held him all night in my arms. Sometimes I didn't sleep, just held him all night in my arms. And I am satisfied with it. I grieve for him. Yes, my pillow at night's never dry—but I'm satisfied to remember. And I would feel cheap and degraded and not fit to live with my daughter or under the roof with the urn of his blessed ashes, those—ashes of a rose—if after that memory, after knowing that man, I went to some other, some middle-aged man, not young, not full of young passion, but getting a pot belly on him and losing his hair and smelling of sweat and liquor—and trying to fool myself that *that* was love-making! I *know* what love-making was. And I'm satisfied just to remember . . . [*She is panting as though she had run upstairs.*] Go on, you do it, you go on the streets and let them drop their sacks of dirty water on you! —I'm satisfied to remember the love of a man that was mine—*only mine!* Never touched by the hand of *nobody! Nobody* but *me!* —Just me! [*She gasps and runs out to the porch. The sun floods her figure. It seems to astonish her. She finds herself sobbing. She digs in her purse for her handkerchief.*]

FLORA [*crossing to the open door*]: Never touched by nobody?

SERAFINA [*with fierce pride*]: Never nobody but me!

FLORA: *I* know somebody that could a tale unfold! And not so far from here neither. Not no further than the Square Roof is, that place on Esplanade!

BESSIE: Estelle Hohengarten!

FLORA: Estelle Hohengarten!—the blackjack dealer from Texas!

BESSIE: Get into your blouse and let's go!

FLORA: Everybody's known it but Serafina. I'm just telling the facts that come out at the inquest while she was in bed with her eyes shut tight and the sheet pulled over her head like a female ostrich! Tie this damn thing on me! It was a romance, not just a fly-by-night thing, but a steady affair that went on for more than a year.

[Serafina has been standing on the porch with the door open behind her. She is in the full glare of the sun. She appears to have been struck senseless by the words shouted inside. She turns slowly about. We see that her dress is unfastened down the back, the pink slip showing. She reaches out gropingly with one hand and finds the porch column which she clings to while the terrible words strike constantly deeper. The high school band continues as a merciless counterpoint.]

BESSIE: Leave her in ignorance. Ignorance is bliss.

FLORA: He had a rose tattoo on his chest, the stuck-up thing, and Estelle was so gone on him she went down to Bourbon Street and had one put on her. [Serafina comes onto the porch and Flora turns to her, viciously.] Yeah, a rose tattoo on her chest same as the Wop's!

SERAFINA [very softly]: Liar... [She comes inside; the word seems to give her strength.]

BESSIE [nervously]: Flora, let's go, let's go!

39

SERAFINA [*in a terrible voice*]: Liar!—*Lie*-arrrrr!

[*She slams the wooden door shut with a violence that shakes the walls.*]

BESSIE [*shocked into terror*]: Let's get outa here, Flora!

FLORA: Let her howl her head off. I don't care.

[*Serafina has snatched up a broom.*]

BESSIE: What's she up to?

FLORA: I don't care what she's up to!

BESSIE: I'm a-scared of these Wops.

FLORA: I'm not afraid of nobody!

BESSIE: She's gonna hit you.

FLORA: She'd better not hit me!

[*But both of the clowns are in retreat to the door. Serafina suddenly rushes at them with the broom. She flails Flora about the hips and shoulders. Bessie gets out. But Flora is trapped in a corner. A table is turned over. Bessie, outside, screams for the police and cries: "Murder! Murder!" The high school band is playing "The Stars and Stripes Forever." Flora breaks wildly past the flailing broom and escapes out of the house. She also takes up the cry for help. Serafina follows them out. She is flailing the brilliant noon air with the broom. The two women run off, screaming.*]

FLORA [*calling back*]: I'm going to have her arrested! Police, police! I'm going to have you arrested!

SERAFINA: *Have* me arrested, *have* me, you dirt, you devil, you *liar!* Li-i-arrrr!

[*She comes back inside the house and leans on the work table for a moment, panting heavily. Then she rushes back to the door, slams it and bolts it. Then she rushes to the windows, slams the shutters and fastens them. The house is now dark except for the vigil light in the ruby glass cup before the Madonna, and the delicate beams admitted through the shutter slats.*]

SERAFINA [*in a crazed manner*]: Have me—have me—arrested—dirty slut—bitch—liar! [*She moves about helplessly, not knowing what to do with her big, stricken body. Panting for breath, she repeats the word "liar" monotonously and helplessly as she thrashes about. It is necessary for her, vitally necessary for her, to believe that the woman's story is a malicious invention. But the words of it stick in her mind and she mumbles them aloud as she thrashes crazily around the small confines of the parlor*] Woman—Estelle— [*The sound of band music is heard.*] Band, band, already—started. —Going to miss—graduation. Oh! [*She retreats toward the Madonna.*] Estelle, Estelle Hohengarten? —"A shirt for a man I'm in love with! This man—is—wild like a Gypsy." —Oh, oh, Lady—The—rose-colored—silk. [*She starts toward the dining room, then draws back in terror.*] No, no, no, no, no! I don't remember! It wasn't that name, I don't remember the name! [*The band music grows louder.*] High school—graduation—late! I'll be—late for it. —Oh, Lady, give me a—*sign*! [*She cocks her head toward the statue in a fearful listening attitude.*] Che? Che dice, Signora? *Oh, Lady! Give me a sign!*

[*The scene dims out.*]

# SCENE SIX

*It is two hours later. The interior of the house is in complete dark-
ness except for the vigil light. With the shutters closed, the interior
is so dark that we do not know Serafina is present. All that we
see clearly is the starry blue robe of Our Lady above the flicker-
ing candle of the ruby glass cup. After a few moments we hear
Serafina's voice, very softly, in the weak, breathless tone of a person near death.*

SERAFINA [*very softly*]: Oh, Lady, give me a sign . . .

[*Gay, laughing voices are heard outside the house. Rosa and
Jack appear, bearing roses and gifts. They are shouting back to
others in a car.*]

JACK: Where do we go for the picnic?

A GIRL'S VOICE [*from the highway*]: We're going in three sail-
boats to Diamond Key.

A MAN'S VOICE: Be at Municipal Pier in half an hour.

ROSA: Pick us up here! [*She races up the steps.*] Oh, the door's
locked! Mama's gone *out!* There's a key in that birdbath.

[*Jack opens the door. The parlor lights up faintly as they enter.*]

JACK: It's dark in here.

ROSA: Yes, Mama's gone out!

JACK: How do you know she's out?

ROSA: The door was locked and all the shutters are closed! Put
down those roses.

JACK: Where shall I . . .

ROSA: Somewhere, anywhere!—Come here! [*He approaches*

*her rather diffidently.*] I want to teach you a little Dago word. The word is "bacio."

JACK: What does this word mean?

ROSA: This and this and this! [*She rains kisses upon him till he forcibly removes her face from his.*] Just think. A week ago Friday—I didn't know boys existed! —Did you know girls existed before the dance?

JACK: Yes, I knew they existed ...

ROSA [*holding him*]. Do you remember what you said to me on the dance floor? "Honey, you're dancing too close?"

JACK: Well, it was—hot in the Gym and the—floor was crowded.

ROSA: When my girl friend was teaching me how to dance, I asked her, "How do you know which way the boy's going to move?" And she said, "You've got to feel how he's going to move with your body!" I said, "How do you feel with your body?" And she said, "By pressing up close!"—That's why I pressed up close! I didn't realize that I was—Ha, ha! Now you're blushing! Don't go *away!* —And a few minutes later you said to me, "Gee, you're beautiful!" I said, "Excuse me," and ran to the ladies' room. Do you know why? To look at myself in the mirror! And I saw that I was! For the first time in my life I was beautiful! You'd made me beautiful when you *said* that I was!

JACK [*humbly*]: You *are* beautiful, Rosa! So much, I ...

ROSA: *You've* changed, *too.* You've stopped laughing and joking. Why have you gotten so old and serious, Jack?

JACK: Well, honey, you're sort of ...

ROSA: What am I "sort of?"

JACK [*finding the exact word*]: *Wild!* [*She laughs. He seizes the bandaged wrist.*] I didn't know nothing like this was going to happen.

ROSA: Oh, that, that's nothing! I'll take the handkerchief off and you can forget it.

JACK: How could you do a thing like that over me? I'm—nothing!

ROSA: Everybody is nothing until you love them!

JACK: Give me that handkerchief. I want to show it to my ship-mates. I'll say, "This is the blood of a beautiful girl who cut her wrist with a knife because she loved me!"

ROSA: Don't be so pleased with yourself. It's mostly Mercurochrome!

SERAFINA [*violently, from the dark room adjoining*]: *Stai zitta!—Cretina!*

[*Rosa and Jack draw abruptly apart.*]

JACK [*fearfully*]: I knew somebody was here!

ROSA [*sweetly and delicately*]: Mama? Are you in there, Mama?

SERAFINA: No, no, no, I'm not, I'm dead and buried!

ROSA: Yes, Mama's in there!

JACK: Well, I—better go and—wait outside for a—while . . .

ROSA: You stay right here!—Mama?—Jack is with me. —Are you dressed up nicely? [*There is no response.*] Why's it so dark in here?—Jack, open the shutters!—I want to introduce you to my mother . . .

JACK: Hadn't I better go and . . .

ROSA: No. Open the shutters!

[*The shutters are opened and Rosa draws apart the curtains between the two rooms. Sunlight floods the scene. Serafina is revealed slumped in a chair at her work table in the dining room near the Singer sewing machine. She is grotesquely surrounded by the dummies, as though she had been holding a silent conference with them. Her appearance, in slovenly deshabille, is both comic and shocking.*]

ROSA [*terribly embarrassed*]: Mama, Mama, you said you were dressed up pretty! Jack, stay out for a minute! What's happened, Mama?

[*Jack remains in the parlor. Rosa pulls the curtains, snatches a robe and flings it over Serafina. She brushes Serafina's hair back from her sweat-gleaming face, rubs her face with a handkerchief and dusts it with powder. Serafina submits to this cosmetic enterprise with a dazed look.*]

ROSA [*gesturing vertically*]: Su, su, su, su, su, su, su, su, su!

[*Serafina sits up slightly in her chair, but she is still looking stupefied. Rosa returns to the parlor and opens the curtains again.*]

ROSA: Come in, Jack! Mama is ready to meet you!

[*Rosa trembles with eagerness as Jack advances nervously from the parlor. But before he enters Serafina collapses again into her slumped position, with a low moan.*]

ROSA [*violently*]: Mama, Mama, su, Mama! [*Serafina sits half erect.*] She didn't sleep good last night.–Mama, this is Jack Hunter!

JACK: Hello, Mrs. Delle Rose. It sure is a pleasure to meet you.

[*There is a pause. Serafina stares indifferently at the boy.*]

ROSA: Mama, Mama, say something!

JACK: Maybe your Mama wants me to... [*He makes an awkward gesture toward the door.*]

ROSA: No, no, Mama's just tired. Mama makes dresses; she made a whole lot of dresses for the graduation! How many, Mama, how many graduation dresses did you have to make?

SERAFINA [*dully*]: Fa niente...

JACK: I was hoping to see you at the graduation, Mrs. Delle Rose.

ROSA: I guess that Mama was too worn out to go.

SERAFINA: Rosa, shut the front door, shut it and lock it. There was a—policeman... [*There is a pause.*] What?—What?

JACK: My sister was graduating. My mother was there and my aunt was there—a whole bunch of cousins—I was hoping that you could—all—get together...

ROSA: Jack brought you some flowers.

JACK: I hope you are partial to roses as much as I am. [*He hands her the bouquet. She takes them absently.*]

ROSA: Mama, say something, say something simple like "Thanks."

SERAFINA: Thanks.

ROSA: Jack, tell Mama about the graduation; describe it to her.

JACK: My mother said it was just like fairyland.

ROSA: Tell her what the boys wore!

JACK: What did—what did they wear?

ROSA: Oh, you know what they wore. They wore blue coats and white pants and each one had a carnation! And there were three couples that did an old-fashioned dance, a minuet, Mother, to Mendelssohn's *Spring Song!* Wasn't it lovely, Jack? But one girl slipped; she wasn't used to long dresses! She slipped and fell on her—ho, ho! Wasn't it funny, Jack, wasn't it, wasn't it, Jack?

JACK [*worriedly*]: I think that your Mama . . .

ROSA: Oh, my prize, my prize, I have forgotten my prize!

JACK: Where is it?

ROSA: You set them down by the sewing sign when you looked for the key.

JACK: Aw, excuse me, I'll get them. [*He goes out through the parlor. Rosa runs to her mother and kneels by her chair.*]

ROSA [*in a terrified whisper*]: Mama, something has happened! What has happened, Mama? Can't you tell me, Mama? Is it because of this morning? Look. I took the bandage off, it was only a scratch! So, Mama, forget it! Think it was just a bad dream that never happened! Oh, Mama! [*She gives her several quick kisses on the forehead. Jack returns with two big books tied in white satin ribbon.*]

JACK: Here they are.

ROSA: Look what I got, Mama.

SERAFINA [*dully*]: What?

ROSA: The *Digest of Knowledge!*

JACK: Everything's in them, from Abracadabra to Zoo! My sister was jealous. She just got a diploma!

SERAFINA [*rousing a bit*]: Diploma, where is it? Didn't you get no diploma?

ROSA: Si, si, Mama! Eccolo! Guarda, guarda! [*She holds up the diploma tied in ribbon.*]

SERAFINA: Va bene.—Put it in the drawer with your father's clothes.

JACK: Mrs. Delle Rose, you should be very, very proud of your daughter. She stood in front of the crowd and recited a poem.

ROSA: Yes, I did. Oh, I was so excited!

JACK: And Mrs. Delle Rose, your daughter, Rosa, was so pretty when she walked on the stage—that people went "Ooooooooooo!"—like that! Y'know what I mean? They all went—"Ooooooooooo!" Like a—like a—*wind* had—blown over! Because your daughter, Rosa, was so—*lovely* looking! [*He has crouched over to Serafina to deliver this description close to her face. Now he straightens up and smiles proudly at Rosa.*] How does it feel to be the mother of the prettiest girl in the world?

ROSA [*suddenly bursting into pure delight*]: Ha, ha, ha, ha, ha, ha! [*She throws her head back in rapture.*]

SERAFINA [*rousing*]: Hush!

ROSA: Ha, ha, ha, ha, ha, ha, ha, ha, ha, ha! [*She cannot control her ecstatic laughter. She presses her hand to her mouth but the laughter still bubbles out.*]

SERAFINA [*suddenly rising in anger*]: Pazza, pazza, pazza!

Finiscila! Basta, via! [*Rosa whirls around to hide her convulsions of joy. To Jack:*] Put the prize books in the parlor, and shut the front door; there was a policeman come here because of—some trouble ... [*Jack takes the books.*]

ROSA: Mama, I've never seen you like this! What will Jack think, Mama?

SERAFINA: Why do I care what Jack thinks?—You wild, wild crazy thing, you—with the eyes of your—father ...

JACK [*returning*]: Yes, ma'am, Mrs. Delle Rose, you certainly got a right to be very proud of your daughter.

SERAFINA [*after a pause*]: I am proud of the—memory of her—father.—He was a baron ... [*Rosa takes Jack's arm.*] And who are *you*? What are you?—per piacere!

ROSA: Mama, I just introduced him; his name is Jack Hunter.

SERAFINA: Hunt-er?

JACK: Yes, ma'am, Hunter. Jack Hunter.

SERAFINA: What are you hunting?—Jack?

ROSA: Mama!

SERAFINA: What all of 'em are hunting? To have a good time, and the Devil cares who pays for it? I'm sick of men, I'm almost as sick of men as I am of wimmen.—Rosa, get out while I talk to this boy!

ROSA: I didn't bring Jack here to be insulted!

JACK: Go on, honey, and let your Mama talk to me. I think your Mama has just got a slight wrong—impression ...

SERAFINA [*ominously*]: Yes, I got an impression!

ROSA: I'll get dressed! Oh, Mama, don't spoil it for me!—the happiest day of my life! [*She goes into the back of the house.*]

JACK [*after an awkward pause*]: Mrs. Delle Rose . . .

SERAFINA [*correcting his pronunciation*]: Delle Rose!

JACK: Mrs. Delle Rose, I'm sorry about all this. Believe me, Mrs. Delle Rose, the last thing I had in mind was getting mixed up in a family situation. I come home after three months to sea, I docked at New Orleans, and come here to see my folks. My sister was going to a high school dance. She took me with her, and there I met your daughter.

SERAFINA: What did you do?

JACK: At the high school dance? We danced! My sister had told me that Rose had a very strict mother and wasn't allowed to go on dates with boys so when it was over, I said, "I'm sorry you're not allowed to go out." And she said, "Oh! What gave you the idea I *wasn't!*" So then I thought my sister had made a mistake and I made a date with her for the next night.

SERAFINA: What did you do the next night?

JACK: The next night we went to the movies.

SERAFINA: And what did you do—that night?

JACK: At the movies? We ate a bag of popcorn and watched the movie!

SERAFINA: She come home at midnight and said she had been with a girl friend studying "civics."

JACK: Whatever story she told you, it ain't my fault!

SERAFINA: And the night after that?

JACK: Last Tuesday? We went roller skating!

SERAFINA: And afterward?

JACK: After the skating? We went to a drugstore and had an ice cream soda!

SERAFINA: Alone?

JACK: At the drugstore? No. It was crowded. And the skating rink was full of people skating!

SERAFINA: You mean that you haven't been alone with my Rosa?

JACK: Alone or not alone, what's the point of that question? I still don't see the point of it.

SERAFINA: We are Sicilians. We don't leave the girls with the boys they're not engaged to!

JACK: Mrs. Delle Rose, this is the United States.

SERAFINA: But we are Sicilians, and we are not cold-blooded.—My girl is a *virgin!* She *is*—or she *was*—I would like to know—*which!*

JACK: Mrs. Delle Rose! I got to tell you something. You might not believe it. It is a hard thing to say. But I am—*also* a—*virgin* . . .

SERAFINA: *What? No.* I do not believe it.

JACK: Well, it's true, though. This is the first time—I . . .

SERAFINA: First time you *what?*

JACK: The first time I really wanted to . . .

SERAFINA: Wanted to what?

JACK: Make—love . . .

SERAFINA: You? A sailor?

JACK [*sighing deeply*]: Yes, ma'am. I had opportunities to!— But I—always thought of my mother . . . I always asked myself, would she or would she not—think—this or that person was—decent!

SERAFINA: But with my daughter, my Rosa, your mother tells you *okay?*—go ahead, son!

JACK: Mrs. Delle Rose! [*With embarrassment.*]—Mrs. Delle Rose, I . . .

SERAFINA: Two weeks ago I was slapping her hands for scratching mosquito bites. She rode a bicycle to school. Now all at once— I've got a wild thing in the house. She says she's in love. And you? Do you say *you're* in love?

JACK [*solemnly*]: Yes, ma'am, I do, I'm in love!—very much . . .

SERAFINA: Bambini, tutti due, bambini!

[*Rosa comes out, dressed for the picnic.*]

ROSA: I'm ready for Diamond Key!

SERAFINA: Go out on the porch. Diamond Key!

ROSA [*with a sarcastic curtsy*]: Yes, Mama!

SERAFINA: What are you? Catholic?

JACK: Me? Yes, ma'am, Catholic.

SERAFINA: You don't look Catholic to me!

ROSA [*shouting, from the door*]: Oh, God, Mama, how do Catholics look? How do they look different from anyone else?

SERAFINA: Stay out till I call you! [*Rosa crosses to the birdbath and prays. Serafina turns to Jack.*] Turn around, will you?

JACK: Do what, ma'am?

SERAFINA: I said, *turn around!* [*Jack awkwardly turns around.*] Why do they make them Navy pants so tight?

ROSA [*listening in the yard*]: Oh, my God . . .

JACK [*flushing*]: That's a question you'll have to ask the Navy, Mrs. Delle Rose.

SERAFINA: And that gold earring, what's the gold earring for?

ROSA [*yelling from the door*]: For crossing the equator, Mama; he crossed it three times. He was initiated into the court of Neptune and gets to wear a gold earring! He's a shellback!

[*Serafina springs up and crosses to slam the porch door. Rosa runs despairingly around the side of the house and leans, exhausted with closed eyes, against the trunk of a palm tree. The Strega creeps into the yard, listening.*]

SERAFINA: You see what I got. A wild thing in the house!

JACK: Mrs. Delle Rose, I guess that Sicilians are very emotional people . . .

SERAFINA: I want nobody to take advantage of that!

JACK: You got the wrong idea about me, Mrs. Delle Rose.

SERAFINA: I know what men want—not to eat popcorn with girls or to slide on ice! And boys are the same, only younger. — Come here. Come here!

[*Rosa hears her mother's passionate voice. She rushes from the palm tree to the backdoor and pounds on it with both fists.*]

ROSA: Mama! Mama! Let me in the door, Jack!

JACK: Mrs. Delle Rose, your daughter is calling you.

SERAFINA: Let her call!—Come here. [*She crosses to the shrine of Our Lady.*] *Come here!*

[*Despairing of the backdoor, Rosa rushes around to the front. A few moments later she pushes open the shutters of the window in the wall and climbs half in. Jack crosses apprehensively to Serafina before the Madonna.*]

SERAFINA: You said you're Catholic, ain't you?

JACK: Yes, ma'am.

SERAFINA: Then kneel down in front of Our Lady!

JACK: Do—do what, did you say?

SERAFINA: I said to get down on your knees in front of Our Lady!

[*Rosa groans despairingly in the window. Jack kneels awkwardly upon the hassock.*]

ROSA: Mama, Mama, *now* what?!

[*Serafina rushes to the window, pushes Rosa out and slams the shutters.*]

SERAFINA [*returning to Jack*]: Now say after me what I say!

JACK: Yes, ma'am.

[*Rosa pushes the shutters open again.*]

SERAFINA: I promise the Holy Mother that I will respect the innocence of the daughter of . . .

ROSA [*in anguish*]: Ma-*maaa!*

SERAFINA: Get back out of that window! —Well? Are you gonna say it?

JACK: Yes, ma'am. What was it, again?

SERAFINA: I promise the Holy Mother ...

JACK: I promise the Holy Mother ...

SERAFINA: As I hope to be saved by the Blessed Blood of Jesus ...

JACK: As I hope to be saved by the ...

SERAFINA: Blessed Blood of ...

JACK: Jesus ...

SERAFINA: That I will respect the innocence of the daughter, Rosa, of Rosario delle Rose.

JACK: That I will respect the innocence—of—Rosa ...

SERAFINA: Cross yourself! [*He crosses himself.*] Now get up, get up, get up! I am satisfied now ...

[*Rosa jumps through the window and rushes to Serafina with arms outflung and wild cries of joy.*]

SERAFINA: Let me go, let me breathe! [*Outside the Strega cackles derisively.*]

ROSA: Oh, wonderful Mama, don't breathe! Oh, Jack! *Kiss Mama! Kiss Mama!* Mama, please kiss Jack!

SERAFINA: Kiss? Me? No, no, no, no!—Kiss my *hand* ...

[*She offers her hand, shyly, and Jack kisses it with a loud smack. Rosa seizes the wine bottle.*]

ROSA: Mama, get some wine glasses!

[*Serafina goes for the glasses, and Rosa suddenly turns to Jack. Out of her mother's sight, she passionately grabs hold of his hand and presses it, first to her throat, then to her lips and finally to her breast. Jack snatches her hand away as Serafina returns with the glasses. Voices are heard calling from the highway.*]

VOICES OUTSIDE: Ro-osa!—Ro-osa!—Ro-osa!

[*A car horn is heard blowing.*]

SERAFINA: Oh, I forgot the graduation present.

[*She crouches down before the bureau and removes a fancily wrapped package from its bottom drawer. The car horn is honking, and the voices are calling.*]

ROSA: They're calling for us! *Coming!* Jack! [*She flies out the door, calling back to her mother.*] G'bye, Mama!

JACK [*following Rosa*]: Good-bye, Mrs. Delle Rose!

SERAFINA [*vaguely*]: It's a Bulova wrist watch with seventeen jewels in it . . . [*She realizes that she is alone.*] Rosa! [*She goes to the door, still holding out the present. Outside the car motor roars, and the voices shout as the car goes off. Serafina stumbles outside, shielding her eyes with one hand, extending the gift with the other.*] Rosa, Rosa, your present! Regalo, regalo—tesoro!

[*But the car has started off, with a medley of voices shouting farewells, which fade quickly out of hearing. Serafina turns about vaguely in the confusing sunlight and gropes for the door. There is a derisive cackle from the witch next door. Serafina absently opens the package and removes the little gold watch. She winds it and then holds it against her ear. She shakes it and holds it again to her ear. Then she holds it away from her and glares at it fiercely.*]

SERAFINA [*pounding her chest three times*]: Tick–tick–tick! [*She goes to the Madonna and faces it.*] Speak to me, Lady! Oh, Lady, give me a sign!

[*The scene dims out.*]

# ACT TWO

*It is two hours later the same day.*

*Serafina comes out onto the porch, barefooted, wearing a rayon slip. Great shadows have appeared beneath her eyes; her face and throat gleam with sweat. There are dark stains of wine on the rayon slip. It is difficult for her to stand, yet she cannot sit still. She makes a sick moaning sound in her throat almost continually.*

*A hot wind rattles the canebrake. Vivi, the little girl, comes up to the porch to stare at Serafina as at a strange beast in a cage. Vivi is chewing a licorice stick which stains her mouth and her fingers. She stands chewing and staring. Serafina evades her stare. She wearily drags a broken gray wicker chair down off the porch, all the way out in front of the house, and sags heavily into it. It sits awry on a broken leg.*

*Vivi sneaks toward her. Serafina lurches about to face her angrily. The child giggles and scampers back to the porch.*

SERAFINA [*sinking back into the chair*]: Oh, Lady, Lady, Lady, give me a—sign . . . [*She looks up at the white glare of the sky.*]

[*Father De Leo approaches the house. Serafina crouches low in the chair to escape his attention. He knocks at the door. Receiving no answer, he looks out into the yard, sees her, and approaches her chair. He comes close to address her with a gentle severity.*]

FATHER DE LEO: Buon giorno, Serafina.

SERAFINA [*faintly, with a sort of disgust*]: Giorno . . .

FATHER DE LEO: I'm surprised to see you sitting outdoors like this. What is that thing you're wearing?—I think it's an undergarment!—It's hanging off one shoulder, and your head, Serafina, looks as if you had stuck it in a bucket of oil. Oh, I see now why the other ladies of the neighborhood aren't taking their afternoon naps! They find it more entertaining to sit on the porches and watch the spectacle you are putting on for them!—Are you listening to me?—I must tell you that the change in your appearance and behavior since Rosario's death is shocking—shocking! A woman can be dignified in her grief but when it's carried too far it becomes a sort of self-indulgence. Oh, I knew this was going to happen when you broke the Church law and had your husband cremated! [*Serafina lurches up from the chair and shuffles back to the porch. Father De Leo follows her.*]—Set up a little idolatrous shrine in your house and give worship to a bottle of ashes. [*She sinks down upon the steps.*]—Are you listening to me?

[*Two women have appeared on the embankment and descend toward the house. Serafina lurches heavily up to meet them, like a weary bull turning to face another attack.*]

SERAFINA: You ladies, what you want? I don't do sewing! Look, I quit doing sewing. [*She pulls down the* "SEWING" *sign and hurls it away.*] Now you got places to go, you ladies, go places! Don't hang around front of my house!

FATHER DE LEO: The ladies want to be friendly.

SERAFINA: Naw, they don't come to be friendly. They think they know something that Serafina don't know; they think I got *these* on my head! [*She holds her fingers like horns at either side of her forehead.*] Well, I ain't got them! [*She goes padding back out in front of the house. Father De Leo follows.*]

FATHER DE LEO: You called me this morning in distress over something.

SERAFINA: I called you this morning but now it is afternoon.

FATHER DE LEO: I had to christen the grandson of the Mayor.

SERAFINA: The Mayor's important people, not Serafina!

FATHER DE LEO: You don't come to confession.

SERAFINA [*starting back toward the porch*]: No, I don't come, I don't go, I—Ohhh! [*She pulls up one foot and hops on the other.*]

FATHER DE LEO: You stepped on something?

SERAFINA [*dropping down on the steps*]: No, no, no, no, no, I don't step on—noth'n . . .

FATHER DE LEO: Come in the house. We'll wash it with antiseptic. [*She lurches up and limps back toward the house.*] Walking barefooted you will get it infected.

SERAFINA: Fa niente . . .

[*At the top of the embankment a little boy runs out with a red kite and flourishes it in the air with rigid gestures, as though he were giving a distant signal. Serafina shades her eyes with a palm to watch the kite, and then, as though its motions conveyed a shocking message, she utters a startled soft cry and staggers back to the porch. She leans against a pillar, running her hand rapidly and repeatedly through her hair. Father De Leo approaches her again, somewhat timidly.*]

FATHER DE LEO: Serafina?

SERAFINA: Che, che, che cosa vuole?

FATHER DE LEO: I am thirsty. Will you go in the house and get me some water?

SERAFINA: Go in. Get you some water. The faucet is working.— I can't go in the house.

FATHER DE LEO: Why can't you go in the house?

SERAFINA: The house has a tin roof on it. I got to breathe.

FATHER DE LEO: You can breathe in the house.

SERAFINA: No, I can't breathe in the house. The house has a tin roof on it and I . . .

[*The Strega has been creeping through the canebrake pretending to search for a chicken.*]

THE STREGA: Chick, chick, chick, chick, chick? [*She crouches to peer under the house.*]

SERAFINA: What's that? Is that the . . . ? Yes, the Strega! [*She picks up a flower pot containing a dead plant and crosses the yard.*] Strega! Strega! [*The Strega looks up, retreating a little.*] Yes, you, I mean you! You ain't look for no chick! Getta hell out of my yard! [*The Strega retreats, viciously muttering, back into the canebrake. Serafina makes the protective sign of the horns with her fingers. The goat bleats.*]

FATHER DE LEO: You have no friends, Serafina.

SERAFINA: I don't want friends.

FATHER DE LEO: You are still a young woman. Eligible for—loving and—bearing again! I remember you dressed in pale blue silk at Mass one Easter morning, yes, like a lady wearing a—piece of the—weather! Oh, how proudly you walked, *too* proudly!—But now you crouch and shuffle about barefooted; you live like a convict, dressed in the rags of a convict. You have no companions; women you don't mix with. You . . .

SERAFINA: No, I don't mix with them women. [*Glaring at the women on the embankment.*] The dummies I got in my house, I mix with them better because they don't make up no lies!—What kind of women are them? [*Mimicking fiercely.*] "Eee, Papa, eeee, baby, eee, me, me, me!" At thirty years old they got no more use for the letto matrimoniale, no. The big bed goes to the basement! They get little beds from Sears Roebuck and sleep on their bellies!

FATHER DE LEO: Attenzione!

SERAFINA: They make the life without glory. Instead of the heart they got the deep-freeze in the house. The men, they don't feel no glory, not in the house with them women; they go to the bars, fight in them, get drunk, get fat, put horns on the women because the women don't give them the love which is glory.—I did, I give him the glory. To me the big bed was beautiful like a religion. Now I lie on it with dreams, with memories only! But it is still beautiful to me and I don't believe that the man in my heart gave me horns! [*The women whisper.*] What, what are they saying? Does ev'rybody know something that I don't know?—No, all I want is a sign, a sign from Our Lady, to tell me the lie is a lie! And then I... [*The women laugh on the embankment, Serafina starts fiercely toward them. They scatter.*] Squeak, squeak, squawk, squawk! Hens—like water thrown on them! [*There is the sound of mocking laughter.*]

FATHER DE LEO: People are laughing at you on all the porches.

SERAFINA: I'm laughing, too. Listen to me, I'm laughing! [*She breaks into loud, false laughter, first from the porch, then from the foot of the embankment, then crossing in front of the house.*] Ha, ha, ha, ha, ha, ha! Now ev'rybody is laughing. Ha, ha, ha, ha, ha, ha!

FATHER DE LEO: Zitta ora!—Think of your daughter.

SERAFINA [*understanding the word "daughter"*]: You, *you* think of my daughter! Today you give out the diplomas, today at the high school you give out the prizes, diplomas! You give to my daughter a set of books call the *Digest of Knowledge!* What does she know? How to be cheap already?—Oh, yes, that is what to learn, how to be cheap and to cheat!—You know what they do at this high school? They ruin the girls there! They give the spring dance because the girls are man-crazy. And there at that dance my daughter goes with a sailor that has in his ear a gold ring! And pants so tight that a woman ought not to look at him! This morning, this morning she cuts with a knife her wrist if I don't let her go!—Now all of them gone to some island, they call it a picnic, all of them, gone in a—boat!

FATHER DE LEO: There *was* a school picnic, chaperoned by the teachers.

SERAFINA: Oh, lo so, lo so! The man-crazy old-maid teachers!—They all run wild on the island!

FATHER DE LEO: Serafina delle Rose! [*He picks up the chair by the back and hauls it to the porch when she starts to resume her seat.*]—I *command* you to go in the house.

SERAFINA: Go in the house? I will. I will go in the house if you will answer one question. —Will you answer one question?

FATHER DE LEO: I will if I know the answer.

SERAFINA: Aw, you know the answer!—You used to hear the confessions of my husband. [*She turns to face the priest.*]

FATHER DE LEO: Yes, I heard his confessions . . .

SERAFINA [*with difficulty*]: Did he ever speak to you of a *woman*?

[*A child cries out and races across in front of the house. Father De Leo picks up his panama hat. Serafina paces slowly toward him. He starts away from the house.*]

SERAFINA [*rushing after him*]: Aspettate! Aspettate un momento!

FATHER DE LEO [*fearfully, not looking at her*]: Che volete?

SERAFINA: Rispondetemi! [*She strikes her breast.*] Did he speak of a woman to you?

FATHER DE LEO: You know better than to ask me such a question. I don't break the Church laws. The secrets of the confessional are sacred to me. [*He walks away.*]

SERAFINA [*pursuing and clutching his arm*]: I got to know. You could tell me.

FATHER DE LEO: Let go of me, Serafina!

SERAFINA: Not till you tell me, Father. Father, you tell me, please tell me! Or I will go mad! [*In a fierce whisper.*] I will go back in the house and smash the urn with the ashes—if you don't tell me! I will go mad with the doubt in my heart and I will smash the urn and scatter the ashes—of my husband's body!

FATHER DE LEO: What could I tell you? If you would not believe the known facts about him . . .

SERAFINA: Known facts, who knows the known facts?

[*The neighbor women have heard the argument and begin to crowd around, muttering in shocked whispers at Serafina's lack of respect.*]

FATHER DE LEO: [*frightened*]: Lasciatemi, lasciatemi stare!—Oh, Serafina, I am too old for this—please!—Everybody is . . .

SERAFINA [*in a fierce, hissing whisper*]: Nobody knew my rose of the world but me and now they can lie because the rose ain't living. They want the marble urn broken; they want me to smash it. They want the rose ashes scattered because I had too much glory. They don't want glory like *that* in nobody's heart. They want—mouse-squeaking!—known facts. —Who knows the known facts?

You—padres—wear black because of the fact that the facts are known by nobody!

FATHER DE LEO: Oh, Serafina! There are people watching!

SERAFINA: Let them watch something. That will be a change for them.—It's been a long time I wanted to break out like this and now I . . .

FATHER DE LEO: I am too old a man; I am not strong enough. I am sixty-seven years old! Must I call for help, now?

SERAFINA: Yes, call! Call for help, but I won't let you go till you tell me!

FATHER DE LEO: You're not a respectable woman.

SERAFINA: No, I'm not a respectable; I'm a woman.

FATHER DE LEO: No, you are not a woman. You are an animal!

SERAFINA: Si, si, animale! Sono animale! Animale. Tell them all, shout it all to them, up and down the whole block! The Widow Delle Rose is not respectable, she is not even a woman, she is an animal! She is attacking the priest! She will tear the black suit off him unless he tells her the whores in this town are lying to her!

[*The neighbor women have been drawing closer as the argument progresses, and now they come to Father De Leo's rescue and assist him to get away from Serafina, who is on the point of attaching him bodily. He cries out, "Officer! Officer!" but the women drag Serafina from him and lead him away with comforting murmurs.*]

SERAFINA [*striking her wrists together*]: Yes, it's me, it's me!! Lock me up, lock me, lock me up! Or I will—*smash!*—the marble . . . [*She throws her head far back and presses her fists to her eyes. Then she rushes crazily to the steps and falls across them.*]

ASSUNTA: Serafina! Figlia! Figlia! Andiamo a casa!

SERAFINA: Leave me alone, old woman.

[*She returns slowly to the porch steps, and sinks down on them, sitting like a tired man, her knees spread apart and her head cupped in her hands. The children steal back around the house. A little boy shoots a beanshooter at her. She starts up with a cry. The children scatter, shrieking. She sinks back down on the steps, then leans back, staring up at the sky, her body rocking.*]

SERAFINA: Oh, Lady, Lady, Lady, give me a sign!

[*As if in mocking answer, a novelty salesman appears and approaches the porch. He is a fat man in a seersucker suit and a straw hat with a yellow, red and purple band. His face is beet-red and great moons of sweat have soared through the armpits of his jacket. His shirt is lavender, and his tie, pale blue with great yellow polka dots, is a butterfly bow. His entrance is accompanied by a brief, satiric strain of music.*]

THE SALESMAN: Good afternoon, lady. [*She looks up slowly. The salesman talks sweetly, as if reciting a prayer.*] I got a little novelty here which I am offering to just a few lucky people at what we call an introductory price. Know what I mean? Not a regular price but a price which is less than what it costs to manufacture the article, a price we are making for the sake of introducing the product in the Gulf Coast territory. Lady, this thing here that I'm droppin' right in youah lap is bigger than television; it's going to revolutionize the domestic life of America. —Now I don't do house to house canvassing. I sell directly to merchants but when I stopped over there to have my car serviced, I seen you taking the air on the steps and I thought I would just drop over and . . .

[*There is the sound of a big truck stopping on the highway, and a man's voice, Alvaro's, is heard, shouting.*]

ALVARO: Hey! Hey, you road hog!

THE SALESMAN [*taking a sample out of his bag*]: Now, lady, this little article has a deceptive appearance. First of all, I want you to notice how *compact* it is. It takes up no more space than . . .

[*Alvaro comes down from the embankment. He is about twenty-five years old, dark and very good-looking. He is one of those Mediterranean types that resemble glossy young bulls. He is short in stature, has a massively sculptural torso and bluish-black curls. His face and manner are clownish; he has a charming awkwardness. There is a startling, improvised air about him; he frequently seems surprised at his own speeches and actions, as though he had not at all anticipated them. At the moment when we first hear his voice the sound of timpani begins, at first very pianissimo, but building up as he approaches, till it reaches a vibrant climax with his appearance to Serafina beside the house.*]

ALVARO: Hey.

THE SALESMAN [*without glancing at him*]: Hay is for horses!— Now, madam, you see what happens when I press this button?

[*The article explodes in Serafina's face. She slaps it away with an angry cry. At the same time Alvaro advances, trembling with rage, to the porch steps. He is sweating and stammering with pent-up fury at a world of frustrations which are temporarily localized in the gross figure of this salesman.*]

ALVARO: Hey, you! Come here! What the hell's the idea, back there at that curve? You make me drive off the highway!

THE SALESMAN [*to Serafina*]: Excuse me for just one minute. [*He wheels menacingly about to face Alvaro.*] Is something giving you gas pains, Maccaroni?

ALVARO: My name is not Maccaroni.

THE SALESMAN: All right. Spaghetti.

ALVARO [*almost sobbing with passion*]: I am not maccaroni. I am not spaghetti. I am a human being that drives a truck of bananas. I drive a truck of bananas for the Southern Fruit Company for a living, not to play cowboys and Indians on no highway with no rotten road hog. You got a four-lane highway between Pass Christian and here. I give you the sign to pass me. You tail me and give me the horn. You yell "Wop" at me and "Dago." "Move over, Wop, move over, Dago." Then at the goddam curve, you go pass me and make me drive off the highway and yell back "Son of a bitch of a Dago!" I don't like that, no, no! And I am glad you stop here. Take the cigar from your mouth, take out the cigar!

THE SALESMAN: Take it out for me, greaseball.

ALVARO: If I take it out I will push it down your throat. I got three dependents! If I fight, I get fired, but I will fight and get fired. Take out the cigar!

[*Spectators begin to gather at the edge of the scene. Serafina stares at the truck driver, her eyes like a somnambule's. All at once she utters a low cry and seems about to fall.*]

ALVARO: Take out the cigar, take out, take out the cigar!

[*He snatches the cigar from the salesman's mouth and the salesman brings his knee up violently into Alvaro's groin. Bending double and retching with pain, Alvaro staggers over to the porch.*]

THE SALESMAN [*shouting, as he goes off*]: I got your license number, Maccaroni! I know your boss!

ALVARO [*howling*]: Drop dead! [*He suddenly staggers up the steps.*] Lady, lady, I got to go in the house!

[*As soon as he enters, he bursts into rending sobs, leaning against a wall and shaking convulsively. The spectators outside laugh as they scatter. Serafina slowly enters the house. The screen door rasps loudly on its rusty springs as she lets it swing gradually shut behind her, her eyes remaining fixed with a look of stupefied wonder upon the sobbing figure of the truck driver. We must understand her profound unconscious response to this sudden contact with distress as acute as her own. There is a long pause as the screen door makes its whining, catlike noise swinging shut by degrees.*]

SERAFINA: Somebody's—in my house? [*Finally, in a hoarse, tremulous whisper.*] What are you—doing in here? Why have you—come in my house?

ALVARO: Oh, lady—leave me alone!—Please—now!

SERAFINA: You—got no business—in here . . .

ALVARO: I got to cry after a fight. I'm sorry, lady. I . . .

[*The sobs still shake him. He leans on a dummy.*]

SERAFINA: Don't lean on my dummy. Sit down if you can't stand up. —What is the matter with you?

ALVARO: I always cry after a fight. But I don't want people to see me. It's not like a man. [*There is a long pause; Serafina's attitude seems to warm toward the man.*]

SERAFINA: A man is not no different from no one else . . . [*All at once her face puckers up, and for the first time in the play Sera-*

*fina begins to weep, at first soundlessly, then audibly. Soon she is sobbing as loudly as Alvaro. She speaks between sobs.*] —I always cry—when somebody else is crying . . .

ALVARO: No, no, lady, *don't* cry! Why should *you* cry? I will stop. I will stop in a minute. This is not like a man. I am ashame of myself. I will stop now; please, lady . . .

[*Still crouching a little with pain, a hand clasped to his abdomen, Alvaro turns away from the wall. He blows his nose between two fingers. Serafina picks up a scrap of white voile and gives it to him to wipe his fingers.*]

SERAFINA: Your jacket is torn.

ALVARO [*sobbing*]: My company jacket is torn?

SERAFINA: Yes . . .

ALVARO: Where is it torn?

SERAFINA [*sobbing*]: Down the—back.

ALVARO: Oh, Dio!

SERAFINA: Take it off. I will sew it up for you. I do—sewing.

ALVARO: Oh, Dio! [*Sobbing.*] I got three dependents! [*He holds up three fingers and shakes them violently at Serafina.*]

SERAFINA: Give me—give me your jacket.

ALVARO: He took down my license number!

SERAFINA: People are always taking down license numbers and telephone numbers and numbers that don't mean nothing—all them numbers . . .

ALVARO: Three, three dependents! Not citizens, even! No relief checks, no nothing! [*Serafina sobs.*] He is going to complain to the boss.

SERAFINA: I wanted to cry all day.

ALVARO: He said he would fire me if I don't stop fighting!

SERAFINA: Stop crying so I can stop crying.

ALVARO: I am a sissy. Excuse me. I am ashame.

SERAFINA: Don't be ashame of nothing, the world is too crazy for people to be ashame in it. I'm not ashame and I had two fights on the street and my daughter called me "disgusting." I got to sew this by hand; the machine is broke in a fight with two women.

ALVARO: That's what—they call a cat fight... [*He blows his nose.*]

SERAFINA: Open the shutters, please, for me. I can't see to work. [*She has crossed to her work table. He goes over to the window. As he opens the shutters, the light falls across his fine torso, the undershirt clinging wetly to his dark olive skin. Serafina is struck and murmurs: "Ohhh . . ." There is the sound of music.*]

ALVARO: What, lady?

SERAFINA [*in a strange voice*]: The light on the body was like a man that lived here . . .

ALVARO: Che dice?

SERAFINA: Niente.—Ma com'è strano!—Lei è Napoletano? [*She is threading a needle.*]

ALVARO: Io sono Siciliano! [*Serafina sticks her finger with her needle and cries out.*] Che fa?

SERAFINA: I—stuck myself with the—needle!—You had— better wash up . . .

ALVARO: Dov'è il gabinetto?

SERAFINA [*almost inaudibly*]: Dietro. [*She points vaguely back.*]

ALVARO: Con permesso! [*He moves past her. As he does so, she picks up a pair of broken spectacles on the work table. Holding them up by the single remaining side piece, like a lorgnette, she inspects his passing figure with an air of stupefaction. As he goes out, he says:*] A kick like that can have serious consequences! [*He goes into the back of the house.*]

SERAFINA [*after a pause*]: Madonna Santa!—*My husband's body,* with the head of a *clown!* [*She crosses to the Madonna.*] O Lady, O Lady! [*She makes an imploring gesture.*] Speak to me!— What are you saying?—Please, Lady, I can't hear you! Is it a sign? Is it a sign of something? What does it mean? Oh, *speak to me,* Lady!—Everything is too strange!

[*She gives up the useless entreaty to the impassive statue. Then she rushes to the cupboard, clambers up on a chair and seizes a bottle of wine from the top shelf. But she finds it impossible to descend from the chair. Clasping the dusty bottle to her breast, she crouches there, helplessly whimpering like a child, as Alvaro comes back in.*]

ALVARO: Ciao!

SERAFINA: I can't get up.

ALVARO: You mean you can't get down?

SERAFINA: I mean I—can't get down . . .

ALVARO: Con permesso, Signora! [*He lifts her down from the chair.*]

SERAFINA: Grazie.

ALVARO: I am ashame of what happen. Crying is not like a man. Did anyone see me?

SERAFINA: Nobody saw you but me. To me it don't matter.

ALVARO: You are simpatica, molto!—It was not just the fight that makes me break down. I was like this all today! [*He shakes his clenched fists in the air.*]

SERAFINA: You and—me, too!—What was the trouble today?

ALVARO: My name is Mangiacavallo which means "Eat-a-horse." It's a comical name, I know. Maybe two thousand and seventy years ago one of my grandfathers got so hungry that he ate up a horse! That ain't my fault. Well, today at the Southern Fruit Company I find on the pay envelope not "Mangiacavallo" but "EAT A HORSE" in big print! Ha, ha, ha, very funny!—I open the pay envelope! In it I find a notice.—The wages have been *garnishee*. You know what garnishee is? [*Serafina nods gravely.*] Garnishee!—Eat a horse!—Road hog!—All in one day is too much! I go crazy, I boil, I cry, and I am ashame but I am not able to help it!—Even a Wop truck driver's a human being! And human beings must cry . . .

SERAFINA: Yes, they must cry. I couldn't cry all day but now I have cried and I am feeling much better.—I will sew up the jacket . . .

ALVARO [*licking his lips*]: What is that in your hand? A bottle of vino?

SERAFINA: This is spumanti. It comes from the house of the family of my husband. The Delle Rose! A very great family. I was a peasant, but I married a baron!—No, I still don't believe it! I married a baron when I didn't have shoes!

ALVARO: Excuse me for asking—but where is the Baron, now? [*Serafina points gravely to the marble urn.*] Where did you say?

SERAFINA: Them're his ashes in that marble urn.

ALVARO: Ma! Scusatemi! Scusatemi! [*Crossing himself.*]–I hope he is resting in peace.

SERAFINA: It's him you reminded me of–when you opened the shutters. Not the face but the body.–Please get me some ice from the icebox in the kitchen. I had a–very bad day . . .

ALVARO: Oh, ice! Yes–ice–I'll get some . . . [*As he goes out, she looks again through the broken spectacles at him.*]

SERAFINA: *Non posso crederlo!*–A clown of a face like that with my husband's body!

[*There is the sound of ice being chopped in the kitchen. She inserts a corkscrew in the bottle but her efforts to open it are clumsily unsuccessful. Alvaro returns with a little bowl of ice. He sets it down so hard on the table that a piece flies out. He scrambles after it, retrieves it and wipes it off on his sweaty undershirt.*]

SERAFINA: I think the floor would be cleaner!

ALVARO: Scusatemi!–I wash it again?

SERAFINA: Fa niente!

ALVARO: I am a–clean!–I . . .

SERAFINA: Fa niente, niente!–The bottle should be in the ice but the next best thing is to pour the wine over the bottle.

ALVARO: You mean over the ice?

SERAFINA: I mean over the . . .

ALVARO: Let me open the bottle. Your hands are not used to rough work. [*She surrenders the bottle to him and regards him through the broken spectacles again.*]

SERAFINA: These little bits of white voile on the floor are not from a snowstorm. I been making voile dresses for high school

75

graduation.—One for my daughter and for thirteen other girls.—
All of the work I'm not sure didn't kill me!

ALVARO: The wine will make you feel better.

[*There is a youthful cry from outside.*]

SERAFINA: There is a wild bunch of boys and girls in this town.
In Sicily the boys would dance with the boys because a girl and
a boy could not dance together unless they was going to be married. But here they run wild on islands!—boys, girls, man-crazy
teachers . . .

ALVARO: Ecco! [*The cork comes off with a loud pop. Serafina
cries out and staggers against the table. He laughs. She laughs with
him, helplessly, unable to stop, unable to catch her breath.*]—I like
a woman that laughs with all her heart.

SERAFINA: And a woman that cries with her heart?

ALVARO: I like everything that a woman does with her heart.

[*Both are suddenly embarrassed and their laughter dies out.
Serafina smooths down her rayon slip. He hands her a glass of
the sparkling wine with ice in it. She murmurs "Grazie."*
*Unconsciously the injured finger is lifted again to her lip and
she wanders away from the table with the glass held shakily.*]

ALVARO [*continuing nervously*]: I see you had a bad day.

SERAFINA: Sono così—stanca . . .

ALVARO [*suddenly springing to the window and shouting*]: Hey,
you kids, git down off that truck! Keep your hands off them bananas! [*At the words "truck" and "bananas" Serafina gasps again
and spills some wine on her slip.*] Little buggers!—Scusatemi . . .

SERAFINA: You haul—you haul bananas?

ALVARO: Si, Signora.

SERAFINA: Is it a 10-ton truck?

ALVARO: An 8-ton truck.

SERAFINA: My husband hauled bananas in a 10-ton truck.

ALVARO: Well, he was a baron.

SERAFINA: Do you haul just bananas?

ALVARO: Just bananas. What else would I haul?

SERAFINA: My husband hauled bananas, but underneath the bananas was something else. He was—wild like a—Gypsy.— "Wild—like a—Gypsy?" Who said that?—I hate to start to remember, and then not remember . . .

[*The dialogue between them is full of odd hesitations, broken sentences and tentative gestures. Both are nervously exhausted after their respective ordeals. Their fumbling communication has a curious intimacy and sweetness, like the meeting of two lonely children for the first time. It is oddly luxurious to them both, luxurious as the first cool wind of evening after a scorching day. Serafina idly picks up a little Sicilian souvenir cart from a table.*]

SERAFINA: The priest was against it.

ALVARO: What was the priest against?

SERAFINA: Me keeping the ashes. It was against the Church law. But I had to have something and that was all I could have. [*She sets down the cart.*]

ALVARO: I don't see nothing wrong with it.

SERAFINA: You don't?

ALVARO: No! Niente!—The body would've decayed, but ashes always stay clean.

SERAFINA [*eagerly*]: Si, si, bodies decay, but ashes always stay clean! Come here. I show you this picture—my wedding. [*She removes a picture tenderly from the wall.*] Here's me a bride of fourteen, and this—this—*this!* [*Drumming the picture with her finger and turning her face to Alvaro with great lustrous eyes.*] My husband! [*There is a pause. He takes the picture from her hand and holds it first close to his eyes, then far back, then again close with suspirations of appropriate awe.*] Annnh?—Annnnh?—Che dice!

ALVARO [*slowly, with great emphasis*]: Che bell' uomo! Che bell' uomo!

SERAFINA [*replacing the picture*]: A rose of a man. On his chest he had the tattoo of a rose. [*Then, quite suddenly.*]—Do you believe strange things, or do you doubt them?

ALVARO: If strange things didn't happen, I wouldn't be here. You wouldn't be here. We wouldn't be talking together.

SERAFINA: Davvero! I'll tell you something about the tattoo of my husband. My husband, he had this rose tattoo on his chest. One night I woke up with a burning pain on me here. I turn on the light. I look at my naked breast and on it I see the rose tattoo of my husband, on me, on *my* breast, *his* tattoo.

ALVARO: Strano!

SERAFINA: And that was the night that—I got to speak frankly to tell you . . .

ALVARO: Speak frankly! We're grown-up people.

SERAFINA: That was the night I conceived my son—the little boy that was lost when I lost my husband . . .

ALVARO: Che cosa—strana!—Would you be willing to show me the rose tattoo?

SERAFINA: Oh, it's gone now, it only lasted a moment. But I did see it. I saw it clearly.—Do you believe me?

ALVARO: Lo credo!

SERAFINA: I don't know why I told you. But I like what you said. That bodies decay but ashes always stay clean—immacolate!—But, you know, there are some people that want to make everything dirty. Two of them kind of people come in the house today and told me a terrible lie in front of the ashes.—So awful a lie that if I thought it was true—I would smash the urn—and throw the ashes away! [*She hurls her glass suddenly to the floor.*] Smash it, *smash it like that!*

ALVARO: Ma!—Baronessa!

[*Serafina seizes a broom and sweeps the fragments of glass away.*]

SERAFINA: And take this broom and sweep them out the back-door like so much trash!

ALVARO [*impressed by her violence and a little awed*]: What lie did they tell you?

SERAFINA: No, no, no! I don't want to talk about it! [*She throws down the broom.*] I just want to forget it; it wasn't true, it was false, false, false!—as the hearts of the bitches that told it . . .

ALVARO: Yes. I would forget anything that makes you unhappy.

SERAFINA: The memory of a love don't make you unhappy unless you believe a lie that makes it dirty. I don't believe in the lie. The ashes are clean. The memory of the rose in my heart is perfect!—Your glass is weeping . . .

ALVARO: *Your* glass is weeping too.

[*While she fills his glass, he moves about the room, looking here and there. She follows him. Each time he picks up an article for inspection she gently takes it from him and examines it herself with fresh interest.*]

ALVARO: Cozy little homelike place you got here.

SERAFINA: Oh, it's—molto modesto.—You got a nice place too?

ALVARO: I got a place with three dependents in it.

SERAFINA: What—dependents?

ALVARO [*counting them on his fingers*]: One old maid sister, one feeble-minded grandmother, one lush of a pop that's not worth the powder it takes to blow him to hell.—They got the parchesi habit. They play the game of parchesi, morning, night, noon. Passing a bucket of beer around the table . . .

SERAFINA: They got the beer habit, too?

ALVARO: Oh, yes. And the numbers habit. This spring the old maid sister gets female trouble—mostly mental, I think—she turns the housekeeping over to the feeble-minded grandmother, a very sweet old lady who don't think it is necessary to pay the grocery bill so long as there's money to play the numbers. She plays the numbers. She has a perfect system except it don't ever work. And the grocery bill goes up, up, up, up, up!—so high you can't even see it!—Today the Southern Fruit Company garnishees my wages . . . There, now! I've told you my life . . . [*The parrot squawks. He goes over to the cage.*] Hello, Polly, how's tricks?

SERAFINA: The name ain't Polly. It ain't a she; it's a he.

ALVARO: How can you tell with all them tail feathers? [*He sticks his finger in the cage, pokes at the parrot and gets bitten.*] Owww!

SERAFINA [*vicariously*]: Ouuu... [*Alvaro sticks his injured finger in his mouth. Serafina puts her corresponding finger in her mouth. He crosses to the telephone.*] I told you watch out.—What are you calling, a doctor?

ALVARO: I am calling my boss in Biloxi to explain why I'm late.

SERAFINA: The call to Biloxi is a ten-cent call.

ALVARO: Don't worry about it.

SERAFINA: I'm not worried about it. You will pay it.

ALVARO: You got a sensible attitude toward life... Give me the Southern Fruit Company in Biloxi—seven-eight-seven!

SERAFINA: You are a bachelor. With three dependents? [*She glances below his belt.*]

ALVARO: I'll tell you my hopes and dreams!

SERAFINA: Who? Me?

ALVARO: I am hoping to meet some sensible older lady. Maybe a lady a little bit older than me. —I don't care if she's a little too plump or not such a stylish dresser! [*Serafina self-consciously pulls up a dangling strap.*] The important thing in a lady is understanding. Good sense. And I want her to have a well-furnished house and a profitable little business of some kind... [*He looks about him significantly.*]

SERAFINA: And such a lady, with a well-furnished house and

business, what does she want with a man with three dependents with the parchesi and the beer habit, playing the numbers!

ALVARO: Love and affection!—in a world that is lonely—and cold!

SERAFINA: It might be lonely but I would not say "cold" on this particular day!

ALVARO: Love and affection is what I got to offer on hot or cold days in this lonely old world and is what I am looking for. I got nothing else. Mangiacavallo has nothing. In fact, he is the grandson of the village idiot of Ribera!

SERAFINA [uneasily]: I see you like to make—jokes!

ALVARO: No, no joke!—Davvero!—He chased my grandmother in a flooded rice field. She slip on a wet rock. —Ecco! Here I am.

SERAFINA: You ought to be more respectful.

ALVARO: What have I got to respect? The rock my grandmother slips on?

SERAFINA: Yourself at least! Don't you work for a living?

ALVARO: If I *don't* work for a living I would respect myself *more*. Baronessa, I am a healthy young man, existing without no love life. I look at the magazine pictures. Them girls in the advertisement—you know what I mean? A little bitty thing here? A little bitty thing there?

[*He touches two portions of his anatomy. The latter portion embarrasses Serafina, who quietly announces:*]

SERAFINA: The call is ten cents for three minutes. Is the line busy?

ALVARO: Not the line, but the boss.

SERAFINA: And the charge for the call goes higher. That ain't the phone of a millionaire you're using!

ALVARO: I think you talk a poor mouth. [*He picks up the piggy and shakes it.*] This pig sounds well fed to me.

SERAFINA: Dimes and quarters.

ALVARO: Dimes and quarters're better than nickels and dimes. [*Serafina rises severely and removes the piggy bank from his grasp.*] Ha, ha, ha! You think I'm a bank robber?

SERAFINA: I think you are maleducato! Just get your boss on the phone or hang the phone up.

ALVARO: What, what! Mr. Siccardi? How tricks at the Southern Fruit Comp'ny this hot afternoon? Ha, ha, ha!—Mangiacavallo!— What? You got the complaint already? Sentite, per favore! This road hog was—Mr. Siccardi? [*He jiggles the hook; then slowly hangs up.*] A man with three dependents!—out of a job... [*There is a pause.*]

SERAFINA: Well, you better ask the operator the charges.

ALVARO: Oofa! A man with three dependents—out of a job!

SERAFINA: I can't see to work no more. I got a suggestion to make. Open the bottom drawer of that there bureau and you will find a shirt in white tissue paper and you can wear that one while I am fixing this. And call for it later. [*He crosses to the bureau.*]—It was made for somebody that never called for it. [*He removes the package.*] Is there a name pinned to it?

ALVARO: Yes, it's . . .

SERAFINA [*fiercely, but with no physical movement*]: Don't tell me the name! Throw it away, out the window!

ALVARO: Perchè?

SERAFINA: Throw it, throw it away!

ALVARO [*crumpling the paper and throwing it through the window*]: Ecco fatto! [*There is a distant cry of children as he unwraps the package and holds up the rose silk shirt, exclaiming in Latin delight at the luxury of it.*] Colore di rose! Seta! Seta pura!—Oh, this shirt is too good for Mangiacavallo! Everything here is too good for Mangiacavallo!

SERAFINA: Nothing's too good for a man if the man is good.

ALVARO: The grandson of a village idiot is not that good.

SERAFINA: No matter whose grandson you are, put it on; you are welcome to wear it.

ALVARO [*slipping voluptuously into the shirt*]: Sssssss!

SERAFINA: How does it feel, the silk, on you?

ALVARO: It feels like a girl's hands on me! [*There is a pause, while he shows her the whiteness of his teeth.*]

SERAFINA [*holding up her broken spectacles*]: It will make you less trouble.

ALVARO: There is nothing more beautiful than a gift between people!—Now you are smiling!—You like me a little bit better?

SERAFINA [*slowly and tenderly*]: You know what they should of done when you was a baby? They should of put tape on your ears to hold them back so when you grow up they wouldn't stick out like the wings of a little kewpie! [*She touches his ear, a very slight touch, betraying too much of her heart. Both laugh a little and she turns away, embarrassed.*]

[*Outside the goat bleats and there is the sound of splintering timber. One of the children races into the front yard, crying out.*]

SALVATORE: Mizz' Dell' Rose! The black goat's in your yard!

SERAFINA: Il becco della strega!

[*Serafina dashes to the window, throws the shutters violently open and leans way out. This time, she almost feels relief in this distraction. The interlude of the goat chase has a quality of crazed exaltation. Outside is heard the wild bleating of the goat and the jingling of his harness.*]

SERAFINA: Miei pomodori! Guarda i miei pomodori!

THE STREGA [*entering the front yard with a broken length of rope, calling out*]: Heyeh, Billy! Heyeh. Heyeh, Billy!

SERAFINA [*making the sign of horns with her fingers*]: There is the Strega! She lets the goat in my yard to eat my tomatoes! [*Backing from the window.*] She has the eye; she has the malocchio, and so does the goat! The goat has the evil eye, too. He got in my yard the night that I lost Rosario and my boy! Madonna, Madonna mia! Get that goat out of my yard! [*She retreats to the Madonna, making the sign of the horns with her fingers, while the goat chase continues outside.*]

ALVARO: Now take it easy! I will catch the black goat and give him a kick that he will never forget!

[*Alvaro runs out the front door and joins in the chase. The little boy is clapping together a pair of tin pan lids which sound like cymbals. The effect is weird and beautiful with the wild cries of the children and the goat's bleating. Serafina remains anxiously halfway between the shutters and the protecting Madonna. She gives a furious imitation of the bleating goat, contorting her face with loathing. It is the fury of woman at the desire she suffers. At last the goat is captured.*]

BRUNO: Got him, got him, got him!

85

ALVARO: Vieni presto, Diavolo!

[*Alvaro appears around the side of the house with a tight hold on the broken rope around the goat's neck. The boy follows behind, gleefully clapping the tin lids together, and further back follows the Strega, holding her broken length of rope, her gray hair hanging into her face and her black skirts caught up in one hand, revealing bare feet and hairy legs. Serafina comes out on the porch as the grotesque little procession passes before it, and she raises her hand with the fingers making horns as the goat and the Strega pass her. Alvaro turns the goat over to the Strega and comes panting back to the house.*]

ALVARO: Niente paura!—I got to go now.—You have been troppo gentile, Mrs. . . .

SERAFINA: I am the widow of the Baron Delle Rose. —Excuse the way I'm—not dressed . . . [*He keeps hold of her hand as he stands on the porch steps. She continues very shyly, panting a little.*] I am not always like this.—Sometimes I fix myself up!—When my husband was living, when my husband comes home, when he was living—I had a clean dress on! And sometimes even, I—put a rose in my hair . . .

ALVARO: A rose in your hair would be pretty!

SERAFINA: But for a widow—it ain't the time of roses . . .

[*The sound of music is heard, of a mandolin playing.*]

ALVARO: Naw, you make a mistake! It's always for everybody the time of roses! The rose is the heart of the world like the heart is the—heart of the—body! But you, Baronessa—you know what I think you have done?

SERAFINA: What—what have I—done?

ALVARO: You have put your heart in the marble urn with the ashes. [*Now singing is heard along with the music, which contin-*

*ues to the end of the scene.*] And if in a storm sometime, or some-time when a 10-ton truck goes down the highway—the marble urn was to *break!* [*He suddenly points up at the sky.*] Look! Look, Baronessa!

SERAFINA [*startled*]: Look? Look? I don't see!

ALVARO: I was pointing at your heart, broken out of the urn and away from the ashes!—*Rondinella felice!* [*He makes an airy gesture toward the fading sky.*]

SERAFINA: Oh! [*He whistles like a bird and makes graceful winglike motions with his hands.*] Buffone, buffone—piantatela! I take you serious—then you make it a joke... [*She smiles involuntarily at his antics.*]

ALVARO: When can I bring the shirt back?

SERAFINA: When do you pass by again?

ALVARO: I will pass by tonight for supper. Volete?

SERAFINA: Then look at the window tonight. If the shutters are open and there is a light in the window, you can stop by for your—jacket—but if the shutters are closed, you better not stop because my Rosa will be home. Rosa's my daughter. She has gone to a picnic—maybe—home early—but you know how pic-nics are. They—wait for the moon to—start singing.—Not that there's nothing wrong in two grown-up people having a quiet conversation!—but Rosa's fifteen—I got to be careful to set her a perfect example.

ALVARO: I will look at the window.—I will look at the win-dooow! [*He imitates a bird flying off with gay whistles.*]

SERAFINA: Buffone!

ALVARO [*shouting from outside*]: Hey, you little buggers, climb down off that truck! Lay offa them bananas!

[*His truck is heard starting and pulling away. Serafina stands motionless on the porch, searching the sky with her eyes.*]

SERAFINA: Rosario, forgive me! Forgive me for thinking the awful lie could be true!

[*The light in the house dims out. A little boy races into the yard holding triumphantly aloft a great golden bunch of bananas. A little girl pursues him with shrill cries. He eludes her. They dash around the house. The light fades and the curtain falls.*]

# ACT THREE

*It is the evening of the same day. The neighborhood children are playing games around the house. One of them is counting by fives to a hundred, calling out the numbers, as he leans against the palm tree.*

*Serafina is in the parlor, sitting on the sofa. She is seated stiffly and formally, wearing a gown that she has not worn since the death of her husband, and with a rose in her hair. It becomes obvious from her movements that she is wearing a girdle that constricts her unendurably.*

[*There is the sound of a truck approaching up on the highway. Serafina rises to an odd, crouching position. But the truck passes by without stopping. The girdle is becoming quite intolerable to Serafina and she decides to take it off, going behind the sofa to do so. With much grunting, she has gotten it down as far as her knees, when there is the sound outside of another truck approaching. This time the truck stops up on the highway, with a sound of screeching brakes. She realizes that Alvaro is coming, and her efforts to get out of the girdle, which is now pinioning her legs, become frantic. She hobbles from behind the sofa as Alvaro appears in front of the house.*]

ALVARO [*gaily*]: Rondinella felice! I will look at win-dooooo! Signora Delle Rose!

[*Serafina's response to this salutation is a groan of anguish. She hobbles and totters desperately to the curtains between the rooms and reaches them just in time to hide herself as Alvaro comes into the parlor from the porch through the screen door. He is carrying a package and a candy box.*]

ALVARO: C'è nessuno?

SERAFINA [*at first inaudibly*]: Si, si, sono qui. [*Then loudly and hoarsely, as she finally gets the girdle off her legs.*] Si, si, sono qui! [*To cover her embarrassment, she busies herself with fixing wine-glasses on a tray.*]

ALVARO: I hear the rattle of glasses! Let me help you! [*He goes eagerly through the curtain but stops short, astonished.*]

SERAFINA: Is—something the—matter?

ALVARO: I didn't expect to see you looking so pretty! You are a *young* little widow!

SERAFINA: You are—fix yourself up . . .

ALVARO: I been to The Ideal Barber's! I got the whole works!

SERAFINA [*faintly, retreating from him a little*]: You got—rose oil—in your hair . . .

ALVARO: Olio di rose! You like the smell of it? [*Outside there is a wild, distant cry of children, and inside a pause. Serafina shades her head slowly with the infinite wound of a recollection.*]—You—don't—like—the smell of it? Oh, then I wash the smell *out*, I go and . . . [*He starts toward the back. She raises her hand to stop him.*]

SERAFINA: No, no, no, fa—niente.—I—*like* the smell of it . . .

[*A little boy races into the yard, ducks some invisible missile, sticks out his tongue and yells: "Yahhhhh!" Then he dashes behind the house.*]

SERAFINA: Shall we—set down in the parlor?

ALVARO: I guess that's better than standing up in the dining room. [*He enters formally.*]—Shall we set down on the sofa?

SERAFINA: You take the sofa. I will set down on this chair.

ALVARO [*disappointed*]: You don't like to set on a sofa?

SERAFINA: I lean back too far on that sofa. I like a straight back behind me . . .

ALVARO: That chair looks not comfortable to me.

SERAFINA: This chair is a comfortable chair.

ALVARO: But it's more easy to talk with two on a sofa!

SERAFINA: I talk just as good on a chair as I talk on a sofa . . . [*There is a pause. Alvaro nervously hitches his shoulder.*] Why do you hitch your shoulders like that?

ALVARO: Oh, that!—That's a—nervous—habit . . .

SERAFINA: I thought maybe the suit don't fit you good . . .

ALVARO: I bought this suit to get married in four years ago.

SERAFINA: But didn't get married?

ALVARO: I give her, the girl, a zircon instead of a diamond. She had it examined. The door was slammed in my face.

SERAFINA: I think that maybe I'd do the same thing myself.

ALVARO: Buy the zircon?

SERAFINA: No, slam the door.

ALVARO: Her eyes were not sincere-looking. You've got sincere-looking eyes. Give me your hand so I can tell your fortune! [*She pushes her chair back from him.*] I see two men in your life. One very handsome. One not handsome. His ears are too big but not as big as his heart! He has three dependents.—In fact he has four dependents! Ha, ha, ha!

SERAFINA: What is the fourth dependent?

ALVARO: The one that every man's got, his biggest expense, worst troublemaker and chief liability! Ha, ha, ha!

SERAFINA: I hope you are not talking vulgar. [*She rises and turns her back to him. Then she discovers the candy box.*] What's that fancy red box?

ALVARO: A present I bought for a nervous but nice little lady!

SERAFINA: Chocolates? Grazie! Grazie! But I'm too fat.

ALVARO: You are not fat, you are just pleasing and plump. [*He reaches way over to pinch the creamy flesh of her upper arm.*]

SERAFINA: No, please. Don't make me nervous. If I get nervous again I will start to cry . . .

ALVARO: Let's talk about something to take your mind off your troubles. You say you got a young daughter?

SERAFINA [*in a choked voice*]: Yes. I got a young daughter. Her name is Rosa.

ALVARO: Rosa, Rosa! She's pretty?

SERAFINA: She has the eyes of her father, and his wild, stubborn blood! Today was the day of her graduation from high school. She looked so pretty in a white voile dress with a great big bunch of—roses . . .

ALVARO: Not no prettier than her Mama, I bet—with that rose in your hair!

SERAFINA: She's only fifteen.

ALVARO: Fifteen?

SERAFINA [*smoothing her blue silk lap with a hesitant hand*]: Yes, only fifteen . . .

ALVARO: But has a boy friend, does she?

SERAFINA: She met a sailor.

ALVARO: Oh, Dio! No wonder you seem to be nervous.

SERAFINA: I didn't want to let her go out with this sailor. He had a gold ring in his ear.

ALVARO: Madonna Santa!

SERAFINA: This morning she cut her wrist—not much but enough to bleed—with a kitchen knife!

ALVARO: Tch, tch! A very wild girl!

SERAFINA: I had to give in and let her bring him to see me. He said he was Catholic. I made him kneel down in front of Our Lady there and give Her his promise that he would respect the innocence of my Rosa!—But how do I know that he was a Catholic, *really?*

ALVARO [*taking her hand*]: Poor little worried lady! But you got to face facts. Sooner or later the innocence of your daughter cannot be respected.—Did he—have a—tattoo?

SERAFINA [*startled*]: Did who have—what?

ALVARO: The sailor friend of your daughter, did he have a tattoo?

SERAFINA: Why do you ask me that?

ALVARO: Just because most sailors have a tattoo.

SERAFINA: How do I know if he had a tattoo or not!

ALVARO: *I* got a tattoo!

SERAFINA: *You* got a tattoo?

ALVARO: Si, si, veramente!

SERAFINA: What kind of tattoo you got?

ALVARO: What kind you think?

SERAFINA: Oh, I think—you have got—a South Sea girl without clothes on . . .

ALVARO: No South Sea girl.

SERAFINA: Well, maybe a big red heart with MAMA written across it.

ALVARO: Wrong again, Baronessa.

[*He takes off his tie and slowly unbuttons his shirt, gazing at her with an intensely warm smile. He divides the unbuttoned shirt, turning toward her his bare chest. She utters a gasp and rises.*]

SERAFINA: No, no, no!—*Not a rose!* [*She says it as if she were evading her feelings.*]

ALVARO: Si, si, una rosa!

SERAFINA: I—don't feel good! The air is . . .

ALVARO: Che fate, die fate, che dite?

SERAFINA: The house has a tin roof on it!—The air is—I got to go outside the house to breathe! Scu—scusatemi! [*She goes out onto the porch and clings to one of the spindling porch columns for support, breathing hoarsely with a hand to her throat. He comes out slowly.*]

ALVARO [*gently*]: I didn't mean to surprise you!—Mi dispiace molto!

SERAFINA [*with enforced calm*]: Don't—talk about it! Anybody could have a rose tattoo.—It don't mean nothing.—You know how a tin roof is. It catches the heat all day and it don't cool off until—midnight . . .

ALVARO: No, no, not until midnight. [*She makes a faint laughing sound, is quite breathless and leans her forehead against the porch column. He places his fingers delicately against the small of her back.*] It makes it hot in the bedroom—so that you got to sleep without nothing on you . . .

SERAFINA: No, you—can't stand the covers . . .

ALVARO: You can't even stand a—*nightgown!* [*His fingers press her back.*]

SERAFINA: Please. There is a Strega next door; she's always watching!

ALVARO: It's been so long since I felt the soft touch of a woman! [*She gasps loudly and turns to the door.*] Where are you going?

SERAFINA: I'm going back in the house! [*She enters the parlor again, still with forced calm.*]

ALVARO [*following her inside*]: Now, now, what is the matter?

SERAFINA: I got a feeling like I have—forgotten something.

ALVARO: What?

SERAFINA: I can't remember.

ALVARO: It couldn't be nothing important if you can't remember. Let's open the chocolate box and have some candy.

SERAFINA [*eager for any distraction*]: Yes! Yes, open the box!

[*Alvaro places a chocolate in her hand. She stares at it blankly.*]

ALVARO: Eat it, eat the chocolate. If you don't eat it, it will melt in your hand and make your fingers all gooey!

SERAFINA: Please, I . . .

ALVARO: Eat it!

SERAFINA [*weakly and gagging*] I can't, I can't, I would choke! Here, you eat it.

ALVARO: Put it in my mouth! [*She puts the chocolate in his mouth.*] Now, look. Your fingers are gooey!

SERAFINA: Oh!–I better go wash them! [*She rises unsteadily. He seizes her hands and licks her fingers.*]

ALVARO: Mmmm! Mmmmm! Good, very good!

SERAFINA: Stop that, stop that, stop that! That–ain't–nice . . .

ALVARO: I'll lick off the chocolate for you.

SERAFINA: No, no, no!–I am the mother of a fifteen-year-old girl!

ALVARO: You're as old as your arteries, Baronessa. Now set back down. The fingers are now white as snow!

SERAFINA: You don't–understand–how I feel . . .

ALVARO: You don't understand how *I* feel.

SERAFINA [*doubtfully*]: How do you–feel? [*In answer, he stretches the palms of his hands out toward her as if she were a fireplace in a freezing-cold room.*]–What does–*that*—mean?

ALVARO: The night is warm but I feel like my hands are–freezing!

SERAFINA: Bad–circulation . . .

ALVARO: No, too *much* circulation! [*Alvaro becomes tremulously pleading, shuffling forward a little, slightly crouched like a beggar.*] Across the room I feel the sweet warmth of a lady!

SERAFINA [*retreating, doubtfully*]: Oh, you talk a sweet mouth. I think you talk a sweet mouth to fool a woman.

ALVARO: No, no, I know—I know that's what warms the world, that is what makes it the summer! [*He seizes the hand she holds defensively before her and presses it to his own breast in a crushing grip.*] Without it, the rose—the rose would not grow on the bush; the fruit would not grow on the tree!

SERAFINA: I know, and the truck—the truck would not haul the bananas! But, Mr. Mangiacavallo, that is my hand, not a sponge. I got bones in it. Bones break!

ALVARO: Scusatemi, Baronessa! [*He returns her hand to her with a bow.*] For me it is winter, because I don't have in my life the sweet warmth of a lady. I live with my hands in my pockets! [*He stuffs his hands violently into his pants' pockets, then jerks them out again. A small cellophane-wrapped disk falls on the floor, escaping his notice, but not Serafina's.*]—You don't like the poetry!—How can a man talk to you?

SERAFINA [*ominously*]: I like the poetry good. Is that a piece of the poetry that you dropped out of your pocket? [*He looks down.*]—No, no, right by your foot!

ALVARO [*aghast as he realizes what it is that she has seen*]: Oh, that's—that's nothing! [*He kicks it under the sofa.*]

SERAFINA [*fiercely*]: You talk a sweet mouth about women. Then drop such a thing from your pocket?—Va via, vigliacco! [*She marches grandly out of the room, pulling the curtains together be-*

*hind her. He hangs his head despairingly between his hands. Then he approaches the curtains timidly.*]

ALVARO [*in a small voice*]: Baronessa?

SERAFINA: Pick up what you dropped on the floor and go to the Square Roof with it. Buona notte!

ALVARO: Baronessa! [*He parts the curtains and peeks through them.*]

SERAFINA: I told you good night. Here is no casa privata. Io, non sono puttana!

ALVARO: Understanding is—very—necessary!

SERAFINA: I understand plenty. You think you got a good thing, a thing that is cheap!

ALVARO: You make a mistake, Baronessa! [*He comes in and drops to his knees beside her, pressing his cheek to her flank. He speaks rhapsodically.*] So soft is a lady! So, so, so, so, so *soft*—is a lady!

SERAFINA: Andate via, sporcaccione, andate a casa! Lasciatemi! Lasciatemi stare!

[*She springs up and runs into the parlor. He pursues. The chase is grotesquely violent and comic. A floor lamp is overturned. She seizes the chocolate box and threatens to slam it into his face if he continues toward her. He drops to his knees, crouched way over, and pounds the floor with his fists, sobbing.*]

ALVARO: Everything in my life turns out like this!

SERAFINA: Git up, git up, git up!—you village idiot's grandson! There is people watching you through that window, the—Strega next door ... [*He rises slowly.*] And where is the shirt that I loaned you? [*He shuffles abjectly across the room, then hands her a neatly wrapped package.*]

ALVARO: My sister wrapped it up for you.—My sister was very happy I met this *nice* lady!

SERAFINA: Maybe she thinks I will pay the grocery bill while she plays the numbers!

ALVARO: She don't think nothing like that. She is an old maid, my sister. She wants—nephews—nieces . . .

SERAFINA: You tell her for me I don't give nephews and nieces!

[*Alvaro hitches his shoulders violently in his embarrassment and shuffles over to where he had left his hat. He blows the dust off it and rubs the crown on his sleeve. Serafina presses a knuckle to her lips as she watches his awkward gestures. She is a little abashed by his humility. She speaks next with the great dignity of a widow whose respectability has stood the test.*]

SERAFINA: Now, Mr. Mangiacavallo, please tell me the truth about something. *When* did you get the tattoo put on your chest?

ALVARO [*shyly and sadly, looking down at his hat*]: I got it tonight—after supper . . .

SERAFINA: That's what I thought. You had it put on because I told you about my husband's tattoo.

ALVARO: I wanted to be—close to you . . . to make you—happy . . .

SERAFINA: Tell it to the marines! [*He puts on his hat with an apologetic gesture.*] You got the tattoo and the chocolate box after supper, and then you come here to fool me!

ALVARO: I got the chocolate box a long time ago.

SERAFINA: How long ago? If that is not too much a personal question!

ALVARO: I got it the night the door was slammed in my face by the girl that I give—the zircon . . .

SERAFINA: Let that be a lesson. Don't try to fool women. You are not smart enough!—Now take the shirt back. You can keep it.

ALVARO: Huh?

SERAFINA: Keep it. I don't want it back.

ALVARO: You just now said that you did.

SERAFINA: It's a man's shirt, ain't it?

ALVARO: You just now accused me of trying to steal it off you.

SERAFINA: Well, you been making me nervous!

ALVARO: Is it my fault you been a widow too long?

SERAFINA: You make a mistake!

ALVARO: *You* make a mistake!

SERAFINA: Both of us make a mistake!

[*There is a pause. They both sigh profoundly.*]

ALVARO: We should of have been friends, but I think we meet the wrong day.—Suppose I go out and come in the door again and we start all over?

SERAFINA: No, I think it's no use. The day was wrong to begin with, because of two women. Two women, they told me today that my husband had put on my head the nanny-goat's horns!

ALVARO: How is it possible to put horns on a widow?

SERAFINA: That was before, before! They told me my husband was having a steady affair with a woman at the Square Roof. What was the name on the shirt, on the slip of paper? Do you remember the name?

ALVARO: You told me to ...

SERAFINA: Tell me! Do you remember?

ALVARO: I remember the name because I know the woman. The name was Estelle Hohengarten.

SERAFINA: Take me there! Take me to the Square Roof!—Wait, wait!

[*She plunges into the dining room, snatches a knife out of the sideboard drawer and thrusts it in her purse. Then she rushes back, with the blade of the knife protruding from the purse.*]

ALVARO [*noticing the knife*]: They—got a cover charge there ...

SERAFINA: I will charge them a cover! Take me there now, this minute!

ALVARO: The fun don't start till midnight.

SERAFINA: I will start the fun sooner.

ALVARO: The floor show commences at midnight.

SERAFINA: I will commence it! [*She rushes to the phone.*] Yellow Cab, please, Yellow Cab. I want to go to the Square Roof out of my house! Yes, you come to my house and take me to the Square Roof right this minute! My number is—what is my number? Oh my God, what is my number?—64 is my number on Front Street! Subito, subito—quick!

[*The goat bleats outside.*]

ALVARO: Baronessa, the knife's sticking out of your purse. [*He grabs the purse.*] What do you want with this weapon?

SERAFINA: To cut the lying tongue out of a woman's mouth! Saying she has on her breast the tattoo of my husband because he had put on me the horns of a goat! I cut the heart out of that woman, she cut the heart out of me!

ALVARO: Nobody's going to cut the heart out of nobody!

[*A car is heard outside, and Serafina rushes to the porch.*]

SERAFINA [*shouting*]: Hey, Yellow Cab, Yellow Cab, Yellow—Cab . . . [*The car passes by without stopping. With a sick moan she wanders into the yard. He follows her with a glass of wine.*]—Something hurts—in my heart . . .

ALVARO [*leading her gently back to the house*]: Baronessa, drink this wine on the porch and keep your eyes on that star. [*He leads her to a porch pillar and places the glass in her trembling hand. She is now submissive.*] You know the name of that star? That star is Venus. She is the only female star in the sky. Who put her up there? Mr. Siccardi, the transportation manager of the Southern Fruit Company? No. She was put there by God. [*He enters the house and removes the knife from her purse.*] And yet there's some people that don't believe in nothing. [*He picks up the telephone.*] Esplanade 9-7-0.

SERAFINA: What are you doing?

ALVARO: Drink that wine and I'll settle this whole problem for you. [*On the telephone.*] I want to speak to the blackjack dealer, please, Miss Estelle Hohengarten . . .

SERAFINA: Don't talk to that woman, she'll lie!

ALVARO: Not Estelle Hohengarten. She deals a straight game of cards.—Estelle? This is Mangiacavallo. I got a question to ask you which is a personal question. It has to do with a very good-looking truck driver, not living now but once on a time thought to have been a very well-known character at the Square Roof. His name was... [*He turns questioningly to the door where Serafina is standing.*] What was his name, Baronessa?

SERAFINA [*hardly breathing*]: Rosario delle Rose!

ALVARO: Rosario delle Rose was the name. [*There is a pause.*]— È vero?—Mah! Che peccato . . .

[*Serafina drops her glass and springs into the parlor with a savage outcry. She snatches the phone from Alvaro and screams into it.*]

SERAFINA [*wildly*]: This is the wife that's speaking! What do you know of my husband, what is the lie?

[*A strident voice sounds over the wire.*]

THE VOICE [*loud and clear*]: Don't you remember? I brought you the rose-colored silk to make him a shirt. You said, "For a man?" and I said, "Yes, for a man that's wild like a Gypsy!" But if you think I'm a liar, come here and let me show you his rose tattooed on my chest!

[*Serafina holds the phone away from her as though it had burst into flame. Then, with a terrible cry, she hurls it to the floor. She staggers dizzily toward the Madonna. Alvaro seizes her arm and pushes her gently onto the sofa.*]

ALVARO: Piano, piano, Baronessa! This will be gone, this will pass in a moment. [*He puts a pillow behind her, then replaces the telephone.*]

SERAFINA [*staggering up from the sofa*]: The room's—going round . . .

ALVARO: You ought to stay lying down a little while longer. I know, I know what you need! A towel with some ice in it to put on your forehead—Baronessa.—You stay right there while I fix it! [*He goes into the kitchen, and calls back.*] Torno subito, Baronessa!

[*The little boy runs into the yard. He leans against the bending trunk of the palm, counting loudly.*]

THE LITTLE BOY: Five, ten, fifteen, twenty, twenty-five, thirty . . .

[*There is the sound of ice being chopped in the kitchen.*]

SERAFINA: Dove siete, dove siete?

ALVARO: In cucina!—Ghiaccio . . .

SERAFINA: Venite qui!

ALVARO: Subito, subito . . .

SERAFINA [*turning to the shrine, with fists knotted*]: Non voglio, non voglio farlo!

[*But she crosses slowly, compulsively toward the shrine, with a trembling arm stretched out.*]

THE LITTLE BOY: Seventy-five, eighty, eighty-five, ninety, ninety-five, one hundred! [*Then, wildly:*] Ready or not you shall be caught!

[*At this cry, Serafina seizes the marble urn and hurls it violently into the furthest corner of the room. Then, instantly, she covers her face. Outside the mothers are heard calling their children home. Their voices are tender as music, fading in and out. The children appear slowly at the side of the house, exhausted from their wild play.*]

GIUSEPPINA: Vivi! Vi-vi!

PEPINA: Salvatore!

VIOLETTA: Bruno! Come home, come home!

[*The children scatter. Alvaro comes in with the ice pick.*]

ALVARO: I broke the point of the ice pick.

SERAFINA [*removing her hands from her face*]: I don't want ice … [*She looks about her, seeming to gather a fierce strength in her body. Her voice is hoarse, her body trembling with violence, eyes narrow and flashing, her fists clenched.*] Now I show you how wild and strong like a man a woman can be! [*She crosses to the screen door, opens it and shouts.*] Buona notte, Mr. Mangiacavallo!

ALVARO: You—you make me go *home,* now?

SERAFINA: No, no; senti, cretino! [*In a strident whisper.*] You make out like you are going. You drive the truck out of sight where the witch can't see it. Then you come back and I leave the back-door open for you to come in. Now, tell me good-bye so all the neighbors can hear you! [*She shouts.*] Arrivederci!

ALVARO: Ha, ha! Capish! [*He shouts too.*] Arrivederci! [*He runs to the foot of the embankment steps.*]

SERAFINA [*still more loudly*]: Buona notte!

ALVARO: Buona notte, Baronessa!

SERAFINA [*in a choked voice*]: Give them my love; give everybody—my love … Arrivederci!

ALVARO: Ciao!

[*Alvaro scrambles on down the steps and goes off. Serafina comes down into the yard. The goat bleats. She mutters savagely to herself.*]

SERAFINA: Sono una bestia, una bestia feroce!

[*She crosses quickly around to the back of the house. As she disappears, the truck is heard driving off; the lights sweep across the house. Serafina comes in through the backdoor. She is moving with great violence, gasping and panting. She rushes up to the Madonna and addresses her passionately with explosive gestures, leaning over so that her face is level with the statue's.*]

SERAFINA: Ora, ascolta, Signora! You hold in the cup of your hand this little house and you smash it! You break this little house like the shell of a bird in your hand, because you have hate Serafina?—Serafina that *loved* you!—No, no, no, you don't speak! I don't believe in you, Lady! You're just a poor little doll with the paint peeling off, and now I blow out the light and I forget you the way you forget Serafina! [*She blows out the vigil light.*] Ecco—fatto!

[*But now she is suddenly frightened; the vehemence and boldness have run out. She gasps a little and backs away from the shrine, her eyes rolling apprehensively this way and that. The parrot squawks at her. The goat bleats. The night is full of sinister noises, harsh bird cries, the sudden flapping of wings in the canebrake, a distant shriek of Negro laughter. Serafina retreats to the window and opens the shutters wider to admit the moonlight. She stands panting by the window with a fist pressed to her mouth. In the back of the house a door slams open. Serafina catches her breath and moves as though for protection behind*] *the dummy of the bride. Alvaro enters through the backdoor, calling out softly and hoarsely, with great excitement.*]

ALVARO: Dove? Dove sei, cara?

SERAFINA [*faintly*]: Sono qui...

ALVARO: You have turn out the light!

SERAFINA: The moon is enough... [*He advances toward her. His white teeth glitter as he grins. Serafina retreats a few steps from him. She speaks tremulously, making an awkward gesture toward the sofa.*] Now we can go on with our—conversation... [*She catches her breath sharply.*]

[*The curtain comes down.*]

*It is just before daybreak the next day. Rosa and Jack appear at the top of the embankment steps.*

ROSA: I thought they would never leave. [*She comes down the steps and out in front of the house, then calls back to him.*] Let's go down there.

[*He obeys hesitatingly. Both are very grave. The scene is played as close as possible to the audience. She sits very straight. He stands behind her with his hands on her shoulders.*]

ROSA [*leaning her head back against him*]: This was the happiest day of my life, and this is the saddest night ... [*He crouches in front of her.*]

SERAFINA [*from inside the house*]: Aaaaaahhhhhhhh!

JACK [*springing up, startled*]: What's that?

ROSA [*resentfully*]: Oh! That's Mama dreaming about my father.

JACK: I—feel like a—*heel!* I feel like a rotten heel!

ROSA: Why?

JACK: That promise I made your mother.

ROSA: I hate her for it.

JACK: Honey—Rosa, she—wanted to protect you.

[*There is a long-drawn cry from the back of the house: "Ohhhh—Rosario!"*]

ROSA: She wanted me not to have what she's dreaming about ...

JACK: Naw, naw, honey, she—wanted to—protect you ...

[*The cry from within is repeated softly.*]

ROSA: Listen to her making love in her sleep! Is that what she wants *me* to do, just—*dream* about it?

JACK [*humbly*]: She knows that her Rosa *is* a rose. And she wants her rose to have someone—better than *me* . . .

ROSA: *Better* than—*you!* [*She speaks as if the possibility were too preposterous to think of.*]

JACK: You see me through—rose-colored—glasses . . .

ROSA: I see you with love!

JACK: Yes, but your Mama sees me with—common sense . . . [*Serafina cries out again.*] I got to be going! [*She keeps a tight hold on him. A rooster crows.*] Honey, it's so late the roosters are crowing!

ROSA: They're fools, they're fools, it's early!

JACK: Honey, on that island I almost forgot my promise. Almost, but not quite. Do you understand, honey?

ROSA: Forget the promise!

JACK: I made it on my knees in front of Our Lady. I've got to leave now, honey.

ROSA [*clasping him fiercely*]: You'd have to break my arms to!

JACK: Rosa, Rosa! You want to drive me crazy?

ROSA: I want you not to remember.

JACK: You're a very young girl! Fifteen—fifteen is too young!

ROSA: Caro, caro, carissimo!

JACK: You got to save some of those feelings for when you're grown up!

ROSA: Carissimo!

JACK: Hold some of it back until you're grown!

ROSA: I have been grown for two years!

JACK: No, no, that ain't what I . . .

ROSA: Grown enough to be married, and have a—baby!

JACK [*springing up*]: Oh, good—Lord! [*He circles around her, pounding his palm repeatedly with his fist and champing his teeth together with a grimace. Suddenly he speaks.*] I got to be going!

ROSA: You want me to scream? [*He groans and turns away from her to resume his desperate circle. Rosa is blocking the way with her body.*] —I know, I know! You don't want me! [*Jack groans through his gritting teeth.*] No, no, you don't want me . . .

JACK: Now you listen to me! You almost got into trouble today on that island! You almost did, but not quite!—But it didn't quite happen and no harm is done and you can just—forget it . . .

ROSA: It is the only thing in my life that I want to remember!— When are you going back to New Orleans?

JACK: Tomorrow.

ROSA: When does your—ship sail?

JACK: Tomorrow.

ROSA: Where to?

JACK: Guatemala.

SERAFINA [*from the house*]: Aahh!

ROSA: Is that a long trip?

JACK: After Guatemala, Buenos Aires. After Buenos Aires, Rio.

Then around the Straits of Magellan and back up the west coast of South America, putting in at three ports before we dock at San Francisco.

ROSA: I don't think I will—ever see you again . . .

JACK: The ship won't sink!

ROSA [*faintly and forlornly*]: No, but—I think it could just happen once, and if it don't happen that time, it never can—later . . . [*A rooster crows. They face each other sadly and quietly.*] You don't need to be very old to understand how it works out. One time, one time, only once, it could be—God!—to remember.—Other times? Yes—they'd be something.—But only once, God—to remember . . . [*With a little sigh she crosses to pick up his white cap and hand it gravely to him.*]—I'm sorry to you it didn't—mean—that much . . .

JACK [*taking the cap and hurling it to the ground*]: Look! Look at my knuckles! You see them scabs on my knuckles? You know how them scabs got there? They got there because I banged my knuckles that hard on the deck of the sailboat!

ROSA: Because it—didn't quite happen? [*Jack jerks his head up and down in grotesquely violent assent to her question. Rosa picks up his cap and returns it to him again.*] —Because of the promise to Mama! I'll never forgive her . . . [*There is a pause.*] What time in the afternoon must you be on the boat?

JACK: Why?

ROSA: Just tell me what time.

JACK: Five!—Why?

ROSA: What will you be doing till five?

JACK: Well, I could be a goddam liar and tell you I was going

111

to—pick me a hatful of daisies in—Audubon Park.—Is that what you want me to tell you?

ROSA: No, tell me the truth.

JACK: All right, I'll tell you the truth. I'm going to check in at some flea-bag hotel on North Rampart Street. Then I'm going to get loaded! And then I'm going to get... [*He doesn't complete the sentence but she understands him. She places the hat more becomingly on his blond head.*]

ROSA: Do me a little favor. [*Her hand slides down to his cheek and then to his mouth.*] Before you get loaded and before you—before you—

JACK: Huh?

ROSA: Look in the waiting room at the Greyhound bus station, please. At twelve o'clock, noon!

JACK: Why?

ROSA: You might find me there, waiting for you...

JACK: What—what good would that do?

ROSA: I never been to a hotel but I know they have numbers on doors and sometimes—numbers are—lucky.—Aren't they?—Sometimes?—Lucky?

JACK: You want to buy me a ten-year stretch in the brig?

ROSA: I want you to give me that little gold ring on your ear to put on my finger.—I want to give you my heart to keep forever! And ever! And ever! [*Slowly and with a barely audible sigh she leans her face against him.*] Look for me! I will be there!

JACK [*breathlessly*]: In all of my life, I never felt nothing so sweet as the feel of your little warm body in my arms...

[*He breaks away and runs toward the road. From the foot of the steps he glares fiercely back at her like a tiger through the bars of a cage. She clings to the two porch pillars, her body leaning way out.*]

ROSA: Look for me! I will be there!

[*Jack runs away from the house. Rosa returns inside. Listlessly she removes her dress and falls on the couch in her slip, kicking off her shoes. Then she begins to cry, as one cries only once in a lifetime, and the scene dims out.*]

# SCENE THREE

*The time is three hours later.*

*We see first the exterior view of the small frame building against a night sky which is like the starry blue robe of Our Lady. It is growing slightly paler.*

[*The faint light discloses Rosa asleep on the couch. The covers are thrown back for it has been a warm night, and on the concave surface of the white cloth, which is like the dimly lustrous hollow of a shell, is the body of the sleeping girl which is clad only in a sheer white slip.*

*A cock crows. A gentle wind stirs the white curtains inward and the tendrils of vine at the windows, and the sky lightens enough to distinguish the purple trumpets of the morning glory against the very dim blue of the sky in which the planet Venus remains still undimmed.*

*In the back of the cottage someone is heard coughing hoarsely and groaning in the way a man does who has drunk very heavily the night before. Bedsprings creak as a heavy figure rises. Light spills dimly through the curtains, now closed, between the two front rooms.*

*There are heavy, padding footsteps and Alvaro comes stumbling rapidly into the dining room with the last bottle of spumanti in the crook of an arm, his eyes barely open, legs rubbery, saying, "Wuh-wuh-wuh-wuh-wuh-wuh . . ." like the breathing of an old dog. The scene should be played with the pantomimic lightness, almost fantasy, of an early Chaplin comedy. He is wearing only his trousers and his chest is bare. As he enters he collides with the widow dummy, staggers back, pats her inflated bosom in a timid, apologetic way, remarking:*]

ALVARO: Scusami, Signora, I am the grandson of the village idiot of Ribera!

[*Alvaro backs into the table and is propelled by the impact all the way to the curtained entrance to the parlor. He draws the curtains apart and hangs onto them, peering into the room. Seeing the sleeping girl, he blinks several times, suddenly makes a snorting sound in his nostrils and waves one hand violently in front of his eyes as if to dispel a vision. Outside the goat utters a long "Baaaaaaa-aaaa!" As if in response, Alvaro whispers, in the same basso key, "Che bella!" The first vowel of "bella" is enormously prolonged like the "baaa" of the goat. On his rubbery legs he shuffles forward a few steps and leans over to peer more intently at the vision. The goat bleats again. Alvaro whispers more loudly: "Che bel-la!" He drains the spumanti, then staggers to his knees, the empty bottle rolling over the floor. He crawls on his knees to the foot of the bed, then leans against it like a child peering into a candy shop window, repeating: "Che bel-la, Che bel-la!" with antiphonal responses from the goat outside. Slowly, with tremendous effort, as if it were the sheer side of a precipice, he clambers upon the couch and crouches over the sleeping girl in a leapfrog position, saying "Che bel-la!" quite loudly, this time, in a tone of innocently joyous surprise. All at once Rosa wakens. She screams, even before she is quite awake, and springs from the couch so violently that Alvaro topples over to the floor.*

*Serafina cries out almost instantly after Rosa. She lunges through the dining room in her torn and disordered nightgown. At the sight of the man crouched by the couch a momentary stupefaction turns into a burst of savage fury. She flies at him like a great bird, tearing and clawing at his stupefied figure. With one arm Alvaro wards off her blows, plunging to the floor and crawling into the dining room. She seizes a broom with which she flails him about the head, buttocks and shoulders while he scrambles awkwardly away.*

*The assault is nearly wordless. Each time she strikes at him she hisses: "Sporcaccione!" He continually groans: "Dough, dough, dough!" At last he catches hold of the widow dummy which he holds as a shield before him while he entreats the two women.*]

ALVARO: Senti, Baronessa! Signorina! I didn't know what I was doin', I was dreamin', I was just dreamin'! I got turn around in the house; I got all twisted! I thought that you was your Mama!— Sono ubriaco! Per favore!

ROSA [*seizing the broom*]: That's enough, Mama!

SERAFINA [*rushing to the phone*]: Police!

ROSA [*seizing the phone*]: No, no, no, no, no, no!—You want everybody to know?

SERAFINA [*weakly*]: Know?—Know *what*, cara?

ROSA: Just give him his clothes, now, Mama, and let him get out! [*She is clutching a bedsheet about herself.*]

ALVARO: Signorina—young lady! I swear I was *dreaming!*

SERAFINA: Don't speak to my daughter! [*Then, turning to Rosa.*]—Who is this man? How did this man get here?

ROSA [*coldly*]: Mama, don't say any more. Just give him his clothes in the bedroom so he can get out!

ALVARO [*still crouching*]: I am so sorry, so sorry! I don't re-member a thing but that I was dreaming!

SERAFINA [*shoving him toward the back of the room with her broom*]: Go on, go get your clothes on, you—idiot's grandson, you!—Svelto, svelto, più svelto! [*Alvaro continues his apologetic mumbling in the back room.*] Don't talk to me, don't say nothing! Or I will kill you!

[*A few moments later Alvaro rushes around the side of the house, his clothes half buttoned and his shirttails out.*]

ALVARO: But, Baronessa, I *love* you! [*A teakettle sails over his head from behind the house. The Strega bursts into laughter. Despairingly, Alvaro retreats, tucking his shirttails in and shaking his head.*] Baronessa, Baronessa, I love you!

[*As Alvaro runs off, the Strega is heard cackling:*]

THE STREGA'S VOICE: The Wops are at it again. Had a truck driver in the house all night!

[*Rosa is feverishly dressing. From the bureau she has snatched a shimmering white satin slip, disappearing for a moment behind a screen to put it on as Serafina comes padding sheepishly back into the room, her nightgown now covered by a black rayon kimono sprinkled with poppies, her voice tremulous with fear, shame and apology.*]

ROSA [*behind the screen*]: Has the man gone?

SERAFINA: That—man?

ROSA: Yes, "that man!"

SERAFINA [*inventing desperately*]: I don't know how he got in. Maybe the backdoor was open.

ROSA: Oh, yes, maybe it was!

SERAFINA: Maybe he—climbed in a window . . .

ROSA: Or fell down the chimney, maybe! [*She comes from behind the screen, wearing the white bridal slip.*]

SERAFINA: Why you put on the white things I save for your wedding?

ROSA: Because I want to. That's a good enough reason. [*She combs her hair savagely.*]

SERAFINA: I want you to understand about that man. That was a man that—that was—that was a man that . . .

ROSA: You can't think of a lie?

SERAFINA: He was a—truck driver, cara. He got in a fight, he was chase by—policemen!

ROSA: They chased him into your bedroom?

SERAFINA: I took pity on him, I give him first aid, I let him sleep on the floor. He give me his promise—he . . .

ROSA: Did he kneel in front of Our Lady? Did he promise that he would respect your innocence?

SERAFINA: Oh, cara, cara! [*Abandoning all pretense.*] He was Sicilian; he had rose oil in his hair and the rose tattoo of your father. In the dark room I couldn't see his clown face. I closed my eyes and dreamed that he was your father! I closed my eyes! I dreamed that he was your father . . .

ROSA: Basta, basta, non voglio sentire più niente! The only thing worse than a liar is a liar that's also a hypocrite!

SERAFINA: Senti, per favore! [*Rosa wheels about from the mirror and fixes her mother with a long and withering stare. Serafina cringes before it.*] Don't look at me like that with the eyes of your father! [*She shields her face as from a terrible glare.*]

ROSA: Yes, I am looking at you with the eyes of my father. I see you the way *he* saw you. [*She runs to the table and seizes the piggy bank.*] Like this, this *pig!* [*Serafina utters a long, shuddering cry like a cry of childbirth.*] I need five dollars. I'll take it out of this! [*Rosa smashes the piggy bank to the floor and raises some coins into her purse. Serafina stoops to the floor. There is the sound of a train whistle. Rosa is now fully dressed, but she hesitates, a little ashamed of her cruelty—but only a little. Serafina cannot meet her daughter's eyes. At last the girl speaks.*]

SERAFINA: How beautiful—is my daughter! Go to the boy!

ROSA [*as if she might be about to apologize*]: Mama? He didn't touch me—he just said—"Che bella!"

[*Serafina turns slowly, shamefully, to face her. She is like a peasant in the presence of a young princess. Rosa stares at her a moment longer, then suddenly catches her breath and runs out of the house. As the girl leaves, Serafina calls:*]

SERAFINA: Rosa, Rosa, the—wrist watch! [*Serafina snatches up the little gift box and runs out onto the porch with it. She starts to call her daughter again, holding the gift out toward her, but her breath fails her.*] Rosa, Rosa, the—wrist watch . . . [*Her arms fall to her side. She turns, the gift still ungiven. Senselessly, absently, she holds the watch to her ear again. She shakes it a little, then utters a faint, startled laugh.*]

[*Assunta appears beside the house and walks directly in, as though Serafina had called her.*]

SERAFINA: Assunta, the urn is broken. The ashes are spilt on the floor and I can't touch them.

[*Assunta stoops to pick up the pieces of the shattered urn. Serafina has crossed to the shrine and relights the candle before the Madonna.*]

ASSUNTA: There are no ashes.

SERAFINA: Where—where are they? Where have the ashes gone?

ASSUNTA [*crossing to the shrine*]: The wind has blown them away.

[*Assunta places what remains of the broken urn in Serafina's hands. Serafina turns it tenderly in her hands and then replaces it on the top of the prie-dieu before the Madonna.*]

SERAFINA: A man, when he burns, leaves only a handful of ashes. No woman can hold him. The wind must blow him away.

[*Alvaro's voice is heard, calling from the top of the highway embankment.*]

ALVARO'S VOICE: Rondinella felice!

[*The neighborhood women hear Alvaro calling, and there is a burst of mocking laughter from some of them. Then they all converge on the house from different directions and gather before the porch.*]

PEPPINA: Serafina delle Rose!

GIUSEPPINA: Baronessa! Baronessa Delle Rose!

PEPPINA: There is a man on the road without the shirt!

GIUSEPPINA [*with delight*]: Si, si! Senza camicia!

PEPPINA: All he got on his chest is a rose tattoo! [*To the women.*] She lock up his shirt so he can't go to the high school?

[*The women shriek with laughter. In the house Serafina snatches up the package containing the silk shirt, while Assunta closes the shutters of the parlor windows.*]

SERAFINA: Un momento! [*She tears the paper off the shirt and rushes out onto the porch, holding the shirt above her head defiantly.*] Ecco la camicia!

[*With a soft cry, Serafina drops the shirt, which is immediately snatched up by Peppina. At this point the music begins again, with a crash of percussion, and continues to the end of the play. Peppina flourishes the shirt in the air like a banner and tosses it to Giuseppina, who is now on the embankment. Giuseppina tosses it on to Mariella, and she in her turn to Violetta, who is above her, so that the brilliantly colored shirt moves in a zigzag course through the pampas grass to the very top of the embankment, like a streak of flame shooting up a dry hill. The women call out as they pass the shirt along:*]

PEPPINA: Guardate questa camicia! Coloro di rose!

MARIELLA [*shouting up to Alvaro*]: Corragio, signor!

GIUSEPPINA: Avanti, avanti, signor!

VIOLETTA [*at the top of the embankment, giving the shirt a final flourish above her*]: Corragio, corragio! The Baronessa is waiting!

[*Bursts of laughter are mingled with the cries of the women. Then they sweep away like a flock of screaming birds, and Serafina is left upon the porch, her eyes closed, a hand clasped to her breast. In the meanwhile, inside the house, Assunta has poured out a glass of wine. Now she comes to the porch, offering the wine to Serafina and murmuring:*]

ASSUNTA: Stai tranquilla.

SERAFINA [*breathlessly*]: Assunta, I'll tell you something that maybe you won't believe.

ASSUNTA [*with tender humor*]: It is impossible to tell me anything that I don't believe.

SERAFINA: Just now I felt on my breast the burning again of the rose. I know what it means. It means that I have conceived! [*She*

121

*lifts the glass to her lips for a moment and then returns it to As-
sunta.*] Two lives again in the body! Two, two lives again, two!

ALVARO'S VOICE [*nearer now, and sweetly urgent*]: Rondinella
felice!

[*Alvaro is not visible on the embankment but Serafina begins to
move slowly toward his voice.*]

ASSUNTA: Dove vai, Serafina?

SERAFINA [*shouting now, to Alvaro*]: Vengo, vengo, amore!

[*She starts up the embankment toward Alvaro and the curtain
falls as the music rises with her in great glissandi of sound.*]

# THE DOG ENCHANTED BY THE DIVINE VIEW

(IL CANE INCANTATO DALLA DIVINA COSTIERA)

*The Dog Enchanted by the Divine View* was first produced by the Provincetown Tennessee Williams Theater Festival on September 16, 2008, at the Boston Center for the Performing Arts Theatre in Boston, Massachusetts. The play was directed by David Kaplan; the set design was by Sue Rees; the lighting design was by Megan Tracy; the costume design was by Rita Ryack; the sound design was by Alex DeFazio; and the production stage manager was A.J. Stevenson. The original cast was as follows:

CLARA     Nancy Cassaro
PAUL      Larry Coen

# THE DOG ENCHANTED BY THE DIVINE VIEW

[*Clara, a plump widow of Italian extraction, is seated in a tight-fitting pale blue silk dress in the exact center of a small sofa in the parlor of a shot-gun cottage. The town is on the Gulf Coast of Mississippi. The parlor is brilliantly lighted with three or four lamps in addition to the bulb suspended from the ceiling. It is full of hot colors, pinks, oranges, vivid greens, purples, the palette of Matisse. It is very tacky and yet rather charming. The plump young widow sits like a woman not accustomed to wearing a girdle, but it is not the girdle alone that accounts for her air of discomfort. She has a severe case of butterflies in the stomach, for she is expecting a caller, the first that she has received in nine years of being a widow.*

*Somewhere in the back of the house there is a loud thud and the widow springs up, clutching her middle with one plump hand, thinking that perhaps her caller has hopped in the kitchen window.*]

CLARA: *Who's there, is somebody there?*

CAT [*identifying itself*]: Me-*owwwwww!*

CLARA [*disgustedly*]: —Oh! You! —hunh . . .

[*She sits down more stiffly than ever. It is apparent from her sighs and wrigglings that the girdle has become intolerable to her. She picks up the clock, holds it to her ear. Sets it back down with an air of desperation. Disappears for a minute behind the brilliant green portieres. Her loud grunting sounds and the elastic snap make it evident that she is ridding herself of the constricting garment. While she is so engaged the caller appears in the half-open door framed by a summer sky that is hardly deeper than dusk. Mr. Mangiacavallo is a young truck driver wearing his best suit which is purplish brown and very shiny*] *and a little too small for his powerful shoulders and thighs. With it he wears a pale green satin tie with a hula girl's picture painted on it. He looks in the door with an air of gleeful antici- pation as a child about to enter a candy store with a couple of nickels in his fist. A wide and irrepressible grin appears on his face, which is engagingly clownish.*

*The widow returns with the girdle in her hand and goes directly to a chest of drawers to put it away when Mr. Mangia- cavallo sticks his hand through the door and says:]*

PAUL: BOO!

CLARA: Oh, my God, how you—scared me . . .

PAUL: You didn't expect me.

CLARA: You said at half past. The clock says quarter to.

PAUL: I took a walk over.

CLARA: You didn' come in your truck?

PAUL: Naw. I didn' come in th' truck. The truck looks too con- spicuous after dark.

CLARA: Too conspicuous? Why?

PAUL: It looks like I'd come for business after dark.

*[With no embarrassment whatsoever he bends and picks up the dropped girdle and hands it back to her.]*

PAUL: You musta just took this off. It still feels hot from your body.

CLARA: Hunh. *[She throws it in a drawer and kicks the drawer angrily shut.]* Be careful how you talk here, Mr.—Is it Mangiacavallo?

PAUL: Mangiacavallo is right but righter still would be Paul. Paul and Clara—two names that go good together.

CLARA: That remains to be seen.

PAUL: I got something for you.

CLARA [*suspiciously*]: What?

PAUL: A chocolate box.

CLARA: Aw. Thanks. My daughter's crazy for choc'lates.

PAUL: These are for you, not your daughter.

CLARA [*emphatically and severely*]: Everything that's for me is also for my daughter, Mr. Mangiacavallo.

PAUL: Yeah, but you take a back seat. You're not yet ready to take back seat by a long shot yet. Open the chocolates! Open the box up now.

CLARA: You wanta eat some? *Huh?*

PAUL: I want to see if they're fresh.

CLARA: Alright. You see if they're fresh. I don't want to look at them now, it would make me sick. In hot weather they get so mushy.

PAUL: Each box got a different movie star's picture on it. I picked out Gloria Greene. Do you like Gloria Greene?

CLARA: Naw. You made a bad choice as far as I am concerned when you picked her out.

PAUL: You don't like America's Sweetheart?

CLARA: Naw. I heard she takes dope.

PAUL: America's Sweetheart takes dope?

CLARA: That's what somebody told me who has a girlfriend that used to work there in pictures. She's very sly about it, very dishonest about it. She comes to work in the morning with a French maid and the French maid stands beside her while she's working and holds this rose. But it ain't just a rose. You know what it is? She's got dope powder in it.

PAUL: Dope powder in it? No!

CLARA [*excitedly*]: *Yes, not no*, powdered dope's sprinkled in it! All of a suddenly she puts on one of those smiles and holds out a hand and says, "Oh, oh, give me that rose, that lovely rose!" She takes it and sniffs up the dope!

PAUL: Ho, ho, *this is a joke, ho, ho, this is a crazy story, this is a joke!*

CLARA: I don't think so. They do some peculiar things. Lots of them are Communists, too. But this one takes dope, "Oh, give me that rose," sniff, sniff, "that lovely, lovely rose," sniff, sniff. One time, she says her girl friend told her, she sniffed the rose too much and they had to call the fire engine out to revive her!

PAUL: Ho, ho what a story, what an imagination that girlfriend has!

CLARA: Well, I personally think she wasn't exaggerating about it too much . . .

PAUL: Naw, just ninety percent, that's all.

CLARA: Set down, why don't you set down if you like to, please . . .

PAUL: You got a bright house.

CLARA: What do you mean, a bright house?

PAUL: Three lamps lighted and a light in the ceiling. You're burning up a lot of kilowatt hours.

CLARA: That's okay. You don't have to pay the light bill.

PAUL: Your husband left you well-fixed?

CLARA: I'm fixed well enough. I take in plenty of sewing.

[*They fall silent. He smiles at her steadily, too steadily, with his warm brown eyes. He watches her flushed face with an air of delight and wonder the way that a dog watches a child that is about to throw a rubber ball for him to chase. His hands rest in his lap and hers in hers, but hers are not relaxed there. They keep bounding up explosively as popcorn. She snatches various small objects from the table beside the sofa and examines them as if she were seeing them for the first time and sets them very carefully back down again. He watches every movement with his air of delight and wonder, his mouth hanging slightly open, his head cocked slightly to one side, exactly like a big and excessively friendly dog, which makes the widow less and less comfortable in her brilliantly lighted little parlor.*

*At last having touched everything else on the table, she moves the gold fish bowl, pushing it a little to the left then a little back to the right. His eyes follow this movement with friendly perplexity, and then he says finally:*]

PAUL: You got a bowl of goldfish.

CLARA: Yeah. We got two left. We used to have five of them.

PAUL: Three of them died on you?

CLARA: Three of them had a—disaster.

PAUL: What disaster was that?

CLARA: The cat of a neighbor jumped in the window one day. I work in the back, I sew, I work like a horse back there. I hear this noise but I don't think nothing of it, I think it's something outside, a kid throwing something, a tennis ball at the house. Then all at once something warned me. You know how you get them feelings?

PAUL: Aw. You had an intuition.

CLARA: Yeah, I had intuition. I jumped up and run in the parlor and there she was with the goldfish. Two she'd finished already and started a third one. Two was still flopping a little bit on the carpet. I scooped 'em up and revived 'em in the washbowl. My daughter was broken-hearted. Adored them fish. But I never cared much for 'em.

PAUL: I think they're hungry.

CLARA: What makes you think they're hungry?

PAUL: They go pop-pop with the mouth.

CLARA: That don't mean they're hungry.

PAUL: What does it mean?

CLARA: It means they're simple minded.

PAUL: They got a rock castle.

CLARA: Yeah, they got a rock castle.

PAUL: What do they do with the castle?

CLARA: They just swim in and out of the doors and windows.

PAUL: They never stay in the castle?

CLARA: They got no rooms in the castle, just doors and windows.

PAUL: Oh, the castle is phoney.

CLARA: [*cynically*] Yeah, like everything else. Especially most of the men you meet nowadays.

[*She picks up a plump silk pillow and examines it closely as if she had just discovered a bloodstain on it. She sighs and puts it back down where it was before.*]

PAUL: Why don't you put it *behind* you?

CLARA: What for?

PAUL: Make you more comfo'table.

CLARA: *I'm* comfortable.

PAUL: You don't *look* it.

CLARA: Well, I feel comfortable whether I look it or not.

PAUL: This parlor is blazing with light.

CLARA: Not too much light for me.

PAUL: Don't it make you self-conscious?

CLARA: Nothing makes *me* self-conscious! Does it make *you* self-conscious?

PAUL: Yeah, it does, a little. It's like a stage at a show, a show on a stage, with all this light blazing on it!

CLARA: Nothin' is goin' on here to be ashamed of. *Is* there?

PAUL: No, but why be so *public*?

CLARA: I got *neighbors*. Neighbors got *tongues*, they *talk*! I don't want to give them no topic for conversation! Not about me!—and my daughter. I got a daughter.

PAUL: Yeah, you told me when I delivered the package to you this morning.

CLARA: I got a daughter, fifteen!

PAUL: Yeah, you told me. You must of got married young. I'm thirty-seven. A middle-aged bachelor. I almost got married but stopped myself just in time. I couldn't compete. She was going with a policeman!

CLARA: Maybe you give up too easy. What's a policeman got that you haven't got?

PAUL: Not a thing!

CLARA: Then why'd you give up?

PAUL: There's two kinds of women and I like the good ones better!

CLARA: Aw. That's a different story . . .

PAUL: Can't we—turn out—*one* light?

CLARA: If you are feeling self-conscious, turn out the floor lamp which is over your chair but leave the *other* ones *on*.

PAUL: You know lots of light increases the temperature of a room in summer?

CLARA: Yes, I can see you are sweating so turn out the floor lamp that you are sitting under.

[*He rises eagerly and starts turning out the lamps, one, two, and three, with a great alacrity. She objects at once, half springing up from the sofa with a defensive gesture.*]

CLARA: I said one lamp, not one, two, three! And leave the

overhead on! What do you think this is? The tunnel of love or something on Pontchartrain beach? You turn two lamps back on.

PAUL: Can I leave the overhead off? [*Pause.*] Can I leave the overhead off?

CLARA [*hoarsely*]: Yeah. Leave that one off. We don't need the overhead on.

PAUL: —You got a strange thing about lights!

CLARA: Well, I got nosey neighbors!

PAUL: What d'you think they would think? Are they *evil*-minded?

CLARA: *Very!* —no, I mean . . .

[*He has crossed to the sofa and tries to wedge himself onto it beside her. The following four lines are said quickly.*]

CLARA: You can't sit here. There's not room enough for two people on this sofa. Hey. Turn the overhead light on!

PAUL: You don't want the overhead light on.

CLARA: I do or I wouldn't of said so.

PAUL: I got sore eyes from that light. Let's leave it off, for God's sake!

CLARA: Alright, leave it off, but you sit back over there. I couldn't care less.

[*Paul coughs violently as he sits down in his chair.*]

CLARA: Catchin' a cold?

PAUL: I'm hot. [*Pause.*] Excuse me!

CLARA: —My daughter she had her first real date tonight... yes she did.

[*Her voice is low and husky. As if unconsciously, she reaches behind her and turns out one of the lamps. Only one remains lighted. He leans eagerly forward with an enormous smile.*]

PAUL: A big event in her life?

CLARA: Yeah. In *my* life, too.

PAUL: A big one in your life, too?

CLARA: Yes, my daughter's first date. I married a man that I loved with all of my heart and he's still living in it... He is! Still living in it, as alive as ever!

[*She rises very slowly, all her self-consciousness gone for a moment, and crosses to the window. A guitar is played almost inaudibly as she hesitates before the soft blue window.* Come le rose *is sung very softly.*]

PAUL [*rising*]: You like to stand at the window.

CLARA: I like to look at the sky.

PAUL: I do, too.

CLARA: The only trouble is neighbors.

[*He has come behind her and tentatively rests a hand on the small of her back. She plucks his hand off gently as a leaf fallen on her.*]

PAUL: You got close neighbors. The only protection is to keep the shades down.

CLARA: Then I wouldn't be able to look at the sky.

PAUL [*leaning out of the window*]: Twinkle, twinkle little star!

CLARA: How I wonder what you are!

PAUL: Up above the world so high!

CLARA: Like a—like a *what*?

PAUL: —Like a *diamond* in the sky . . .

CLARA: Yeah, that's right, like a diamond. In the sky. Ha, ha, ha!

[*His hand touches the small of her back again, a little bit lower this time.*]

CLARA: She had on voile, *white* voile . . .

PAUL: Who?

CLARA: My daughter.

PAUL: Oh, we are back on your fav'rite subject again.

CLARA: You think I talk too much about my daughter?

PAUL: No, no, not a bit.

CLARA: It's very funny, the mother and the daughter both having a date the same night. Don't that seem funny?

PAUL: Nothing could be more natural in the world! You are not yet ready to take a back seat, by a long shot.

CLARA: I have been very emotional all day. This is the anniversary of the day that I met my husband.

PAUL: And today you meet me.

CLARA: That is not what I mean.

PAUL: No, but today you meet me! A woman can't live in a grave.

CLARA: I had a crying spell this afternoon. You know how children can be, they are very unfeeling sometimes. I showed her this dress I had made her out of white voile. You know what that girl said to me? "Mother," she said, "you want me to look like curtains in a front window."

PAUL: That was very unfeeling.

CLARA: Oh, she changed her tune when I tried it on her! She was delighted with it when she looked in the mirror. —Don't look now but we're being watched from next door!

PAUL: That's what you get for making the house like a stage! Pull the windowshade down.

CLARA: No, no, wait! Wait until she stops looking. We never speak. One time I caught her husband watching my daughter undress. Can you imagine a dirty old man like that? Watching a young girl undress through a bedroom window?

PAUL: Terrible!

CLARA: Yeah. He come out between the two houses and stood just like a tree! Right there on the lawn between this house and their house, eyes bugging out of his head while my daughter undressed! —She shouldn't of had the shade up, but a girl of fourteen is still innocent in her mind. And ought to stay so. Oh, did I give him "Hail Columbia" when I seen him at it! I happened to be outside myself at that time. And since that time we have never exchanged one word, not even hello!—him or that woman either!

[*He pulls the windowshade down. She pretends not to notice. He faces her with a brilliant smile.*]

CLARA: You like a player piano? This one is an electric, you don't have to pump the pedals. I will put a roll on it. Let's see now. "The Vienna"– [*She has picked up a piano roll.*] –"The

Vienna"—what's that?—*Woods*, oh,—woods—yes, "The Vienna Woods" is a waltz, a real pretty waltz! Let's play it, the piano's electric, it's an electric piano my husband bought before he was— Here, now, let's have some music.

[*She attaches the piano roll. While she is bending over to start it, he comes up behind her and encircles her bent over figure with his arm, at the same time sucking in his breath with great violence.*]

CLARA: HEY! —Somebody's getting *familiar*! Sit back down where you were.

PAUL: One thing that I like about you is you don't wear a girdle, I like that you don't wear no girdle!

[*The piano starts suddenly and very rapidly.*]

CLARA [*shouting above the waltz*]: Is that too loud? Is that too fast or something? Something's wrong with it, it's going too fast or too loud!

PAUL: Turn it down just a little.

[*She bends over to make another adjustment. He reaches out and pokes a finger in the vicinity of her appendix.*]

PAUL: *Soft! Soft!*

CLARA [*knocking his hand away*]: Oh, my goodness, I must of done the wrong thing, it's playing faster.

PAUL: Yeah, you speeded it up.

CLARA: Speed it down a little. Do you know how?

[*They stare helplessly at each other. The piano is very loud and very fast.*]

CLARA [*almost screaming*]: *Fix it, fix it, please fix it!*

[*Without removing his eyes from her face, he reaches out and turns the piano down soft.*]

CLARA [*with a great sigh*]: —That's—better . . . [*Pause.*]

PAUL: No, you don't wear no girdle!

CLARA: Now, Mr. Mangiacavallo!

PAUL: The shade is pulled down—we are two lonely people!

CLARA: Hey.

[*He plants a kiss on her throat.*]

PAUL: Why keep up formalities, why keep formalities up?

CLARA: I am the mother of a fifteen-year-old—girl . . .

PAUL: I loved you the moment I seen you, love at first sight, believe me!

CLARA: Don't be silly.

PAUL: A woman your age is in the prime of her life. You're plump, you're juicy !

CLARA: Hey!

PAUL: Why are you pushing against me? Hold still a minute! Let's get together, now let's just press close together, we don't have to move! We don't have to move if we just press close together for half a minute, no more, that's all's necessary!

CLARA: Oh, now, please!

PAUL: Hold still, now, hold still, now, just a minute!

CIARA: Please, now, *please*!

PAUL: *Hold still.*

CLARA: *No, please!*

PAUL: Hold still, hold still, just let me get closer, just a little bit closer, that's all I need, now, just a little bit closer!

CLARA: No, no, no, no closer, no, closer, no, no, please, now, please now, let me go, now, let me go, now, let—me—GO!

[*The piano roll comes to a violent finish. The paper flies off the roll and there is a loud mechanical noise, a rattle and a swish and a thud.*]

CLARA [*breaking loose*]: The piano is stopped. Those people next door will hear us! What if my daughter comes home? If Rose should come in what would she think of her mother?

[*He plunges towards her, knocking the floorlamp over.*]

CLARA: There, now, you've done it, you've knocked the floor-lamp over!—I have a reputation to uphold in this neighborhood. I am the mother of a fifteen-year-old girl and people have tongues a mile long!—You have broken my floorlamp.

[*She says this between gasps for breath. All this while he is shuffling warily toward her like a boxer preparing for a knock out. His breath is louder than hers and the tip of his tongue protrudes between his teeth.*]

CLARA: What are you trying to do, bite your tongue off like that? I think we better call this night to a halt! Yes, we'd better call a halt to this night, right now, this minute before it goes no further. Good night, Mr. Mangiacavallo. Go home, please! I got a headache and I am upset at my stomach. I might even throw up!

[*She turns and stalks out of the parlor. A door slams in the rear. He sighs and picks up the floorlamp. Then he seats himself upon the piano stool in the attitude of* The Thinker *of Rodin.*

*After a while the voice of the widow is heard from the back of the house.*]

CLARA: Have you gone? Have you gone yet? Mr. Mangiacavallo, have you gone? [*He doesn't answer.*]—Mr. Mangiacavallo—have you—*gone?*

[*Still no answer. Presently she comes into the front room again. She wears a rayon kimono with scarlet poppies on it. She doesn't see him sitting in the dark room. She thinks that he has left. She raises a windowshade and begins to weep very softly and forlornly at the window, looking out into the soft blue night.*]

PAUL [*springing up*]: BOO!

[*She screams as the curtain comes down.*]

# THE DOG AND THE ROSE

A character in Edward Albee's *The Play about the Baby* talks about a time she pestered writers, trying to obtain an understanding of the creative mind. Finally one author spoke to her on the phone and she explained she wanted to spend a few weeks watching him move his words from his mind to the page. She wouldn't bother him, she said, she'd be a mouse. The humor of such a preposterous notion—that one can comprehend the interior act of creativity by watching a writer write—is heightened when the woman indignantly reports the author's response to her plea: "I'd rather die," he said, and hung up.

Perhaps the closest we can come to seeing the creative process of authors is to study their evolving artistic intention as it is revealed in successive drafts of their work. In addition to *The Rose Tattoo*, this volume contains the first trade publication of Tennessee Williams's one-act play, *The Dog Enchanted by the Divine View*. It is, according to Brian Parker, who has done an exhaustive provisional study of all the known drafts, alternatives, and revisions of *The Rose Tattoo*, the earliest version. Williams noted parenthetically on the typescript that it is "A 1-act sketch from which 'The Rose Tattoo' was derived." An earlier one-act play, *A Perfect Analysis Given By A Parrot,* is not really a version of *The Rose Tattoo,* but rather a comic scene between two women, Bessie and Flora, imported by Williams into *The Rose Tattoo* where they serve several functions. They prevent Serafina from attending her daughter's graduation; they show again Serafina's reverence for the memory of her husband by her objection to their "man-crazy" talk in the same room with his ashes; and they underline by their anti-Italian epithets (along with those of the Salesman and the Strega) the Sicilian otherness of Serafina and Alvaro in America. Probably their most important function in *The Rose Tattoo* is to expose Serafina to the gossip about her husband's ongoing affair with Estelle Hohengarten the year before his death. While *Parrot's* protagonists are peripheral if important in *The Rose Tattoo,* the protagonists of *Dog Enchanted,* Clara and Paul, are versions of *The Rose Tattoo*'s main characters, Serafina delle Rose and Alvaro Mangiacavallo. It is striking that, after all the visions and revisions that went into *The Rose Tattoo,* the core drama of the one-act *Dog Enchanted*—the conflict within a woman about whether to accept a new love in her life—remains the core drama of the three-act *The Rose Tattoo*. While *Dog Enchanted* leaves the possibility of sex and a relationship between Paul and Clara up in the air, in *The Rose Tattoo* Serafina and Alvaro spend the night together and, in the end, Serafina goes to join Alvaro, shouting her love.

Clara's mention of her daughter in *Dog Enchanted* blossoms into a whole mirroring subplot in *The Rose Tattoo,* for just as Serafina goes after Alvaro, so too Rosa goes off, with her mother's blessing finally, to be with her young sailor, Jack. There is something of Williams's sister Rose in his creation of the character Rosa: in his *Memoirs* Williams described his "highly sexed" sister as "tearing herself apart mentally and physically" by the repressions "imposed upon her" by their mother's Puritanism. Although Rosa's name is part of a ubiquitous rose imagery in *The Rose Tattoo,* there are only two mentions of roses in *Dog Enchanted*. The first is in the conversation between Paul and Clara about the actress Gloria Greene possibly sniffing roses with dope powder sprinkled on them (which may call to mind Serafina's husband, Rosario, trucking bananas with dope hidden under them). The second is the stage direction that tells of "*Come le rose*" being sung softly after Clara mentions that her dead husband still lives in her heart. Gaetano Lama's song is apt, for it contrasts the roses of the present with the now faded roses of the past: the present roses are not as meaningful to the singer as the roses of the past once were, but the roses of the past are gone. Something of this idea gets into *The Rose Tattoo* when Rosa tells Jack that nothing will ever compare with first love, and when Alvaro—with his clownish head and smaller banana truck—falls short in comparison to Serafina's late husband, Rosario.

When Clara tells Paul it is the anniversary of the day she met her now dead husband, Paul tells her, "A woman can't live in a grave." This prefigures Alvaro's words to Serafina, "you have put your heart in the marble urn with the ashes." There is no straight line between *Dog Enchanted* and *The Rose Tattoo*—the drafts in between show Williams trying out many possibilities for the title, the plot, the ending; but what is consistent is the tension the female protagonist feels between an idealized dead past and a vital if imperfect present reality, between desire for respectability and a need to break free of its chains, and between spiritual yearning and an animal nature. The latter is present in the very title of *The Dog Enchanted by the Divine View*. Williams hand-wrote an alternate title on his typescript in rough Italian, *Il Canne Incantade delle Divina Costiere*, which has been corrected to *Il Cane Incantato dalla Divina Costiera*, literally "The Dog Enchanted by the Divine Coastline." Twice in *Dog Enchanted* Paul is likened to a dog when he is looking at Clara—she is his divine view and coastline, her plump curves filling him with delight. But Clara too is enchanted by a heavenly view—of stars in the sky (paralleled by Serafina's gaze on her statue of the Madonna "in a starry blue robe") —and her contrasting animal nature is suggested when her voice gets "low and husky" as she turns out one of the lights. Paul in *Dog*

*Enchanted* has the same surname as Alvaro, "Mangiacavallo," which Alvaro explains means in Italian "Eat a horse." We can assume it is Paul's appetite for the "juicy" Clara that prompts him to call on her, and surely it is no accident that Williams has Clara say she works "like a horse." The eating metaphor is also present in the discussion of her cat having eaten three of her goldfish. Paul is associated with the cat when, at the beginning of the play, Clara mistakes its entrance for his (and its entrance is immediately followed by his). In *The Rose Tattoo* an animal aspect of human nature is symbolized in the goat which keeps breaking free: when Alvaro chases it, Serafina "gives a furious imitation of the bleating goat... It is the fury of woman at the desire she suffers." When Alvaro stumbles upon the sleeping Rosa, he is overcome by her beauty, repeating "*Che bella!*"–stage directions instruct that the first vowel of "*bella*" should be "enormously prolonged like the 'baaa' of the goat" bleating outside. In effect, Alvaro metaphorically becomes a goat enchanted by a divine view.

In his essay, "The Meaning of *The Rose Tattoo*," Williams says the play "is the Dionysian element in human life, its mystery, its beauty, its significance." But he cautions that, "although the goat is one of its immemorial symbols, it must not be confused with mere sexuality." Its "purest form," he posits, is revealed in the flight of birds, children at play, and the artist's desire to go beyond the bounds of what has been done before. Children at play feature prominently in *The Rose Tattoo*, as does birdflight in Alvaro's cry of "*Rondinella Felice!*" However it is not something within the play but the play itself, as Williams's first full-length comedy, that exemplifies the artist's desire to go beyond what he had done before. He was working on a number of dramatic projects in December, 1948, but the only one that had "any fire in it," he wrote in a notebook, was the one "I was just playing with for my own entertainment" (i.e., a draft of *The Rose Tattoo*). "The trouble is," he continued, "that I am being bullied and intimidated by my own success and the fame that surrounds it and what people expect of me and their demands on me." There might be safety in doing what others expect, but that would put him in danger of artistic death. "Don't play it safe," he recalls Irene Selznick warning him.

The story of Serafina delle Rose can be considered a personal allegory for Williams not just in his need for artistic freedom, but also in his need to be himself, as a gay man. Serafina's breaking free of restraints to grasp love parallels Williams's choice to live his life despite society's disapproval. *The Rose Tattoo* is dedicated "To Frank in return for Sicily," and in his *Memoirs* Williams called it his "love-play to the world," remarking that it "was permeated with the happy young love for Frankie." Frankie was Frank Merlo, a first-generation Sicilian American and one-time truck driver and sailor who, in late 1948, began a fourteen-year relationship with Williams. In a letter to Elia Kazan written in June of 1950, Williams said that he was "going to be a great deal more unguarded than I have ever been in the past and I am going to tell you a lot about myself and my life." The gist of what he had to say about his life was that during the past two years he had been, for the first time, "happy and at home with someone," and that he thought of *The Rose Tattoo* "as a monument to that happiness, a house built of images and words for that happiness to live in." The surname Mangiacavallo is a play on Williams's nickname, "Little Horse," for Merlo, the person with whom he had been happy and at home. In some drafts of the play, Alvaro's surname is Merlo, not Mangiacavallo. Williams and Merlo lived together in Rome for part of 1949, and Merlo was Williams's guide during a trip through Sicily, where Merlo still had family relations: Taormina, Catania, Palermo, Cefalù—Williams was enchanted. In contrast to the puritanical atmosphere in the Cold War United States of that period, in which the 81$^{st}$ Congress officially declared homosexuals to be "sex perverts," Italy was associated in Williams's mind with what he called "total freedom of life." Young Italian men, he wrote in his *Memoirs*, "are raised without any of our puritanical reserves about sex." With Italian friends, such as Anna Magnani (who later played Serafina in the film version of *The Rose Tattoo*), he could be completely open about his relationship with Merlo.

Another essay by Williams, the one that originally prefaced *The Rose Tattoo*, suggests just how much of an experiment his comedy is. In "The Timeless World of a Play" he writes of "a certain foolery, a certain distortion toward the grotesque," as a possible solution for the playwright, to get around the modern audience's immersion in the rush of time and its consequent numbness of compassion. The contemporary playwright must somehow work a sense of time into the timeless world he creates, so that world will not seem false to his audience. Although Williams does not mention *The Rose Tattoo,* this essay illuminates his thinking while writing it, not only because he worked a symbol of time into the play, the motif of Rosa never getting Serafina's graduation gift of a wrist watch because of the rush of events, but also because in *The Rose Tattoo* Williams experimented with the grotesque. We can rejoice in the determination of Serafina and her daughter to seize the day, and so the play's conclusion is a happy event *sub specie aeternitatis*, but that ending is in the context of a world of grotesquerie, and in such a world pratfalls are always waiting to come on stage. So we also feel the ending as an occasion in the flow of time.

It is understandable that Williams would set *The Rose Tattoo* in a Sicilian-American community. "We are Sicilians," Serafina tells Rosa's Jack, "we are not cold-blooded." And Jack tells her, "Mrs. Delle Rose, I guess that Sicilians are very emotional people." Passionate characters are a natural for drama, and for the comic grotesque. Whether the grotesque is experienced as comic or tragic depends upon aesthetic distance. In her book, *Five O'Clock Angel*, Maria St. Just tells the following anecdote:

Merlo's immediate relations were an enormous brood of first-generation Sicilian immigrants who had settled in New Jersey or somewhere. His poor mother was tormented by the size and vociferousness of her family, and used often, after arguments, to climb the fig tree in the backyard and sulk, sometimes for hours on end. I remember Frankie telling us that after one particularly blinding row, she refused to come down. Having shouted at her, and pleaded with her, her sons eventually took an axe to the tree and brought the whole thing down, with her in it. Tennessee and I, hearing this story, were whimpering with laughter. Frankie was livid: he took her very seriously indeed.

There is plenty of grotesquerie in *The Rose Tattoo*, and the stage directions even use the word a few times to describe the goings on. One of those times is Alvaro's "grotesquely violent and comic" wooing of Serafina during which he knocks over a lamp, as does Paul in *Dog Enchanted* during his pursuit of Clara. At one point, according to the stage directions, "Alvaro becomes tremulously pleading, shuffling forward a little, slightly crouched like a beggar." Compare this with the perhaps even more comically grotesque pursuit of Clara by Paul: "He is shuffling warily toward her like a boxer preparing for a knock out. His breath is louder than hers and the tip of his tongue protrudes between his teeth." Paul's ardor in *Dog Enchanted* is expressed gracelessly when he says, "We don't have to move if we just press close together for half a minute, no more, that's all's necessary!" And a few moments later, "that's all I need." This matches in awkwardness the moment in *The Rose Tattoo* when Alvaro talks of wanting "the sweet warmth of a lady" in his life, only to have a condom drop from his pocket. "Is that a piece of the poetry that you dropped out of your pocket?" Serafina sarcastically asks. She is no whore ("*Io, non sono puttana!"*), she says, and calls Alvaro a filthy lowlife (*"sporcaccione,"* she cries, *"Vigliacco!"*), while he presses his cheek to her flank, "rhapsodically" murmuring, "So soft is a lady! So, so, so, so, so, soft—is a lady!" Our laughter is not just at Alvaro and Serafina, and Paul and Clara; it is the laughter that recognizes ourselves in our own awkward moments, the incongruities of the human condition in this imperfect world. We aspire to poetry, and fall on our face, or some other body part. Rosa describes the elegance of her school graduation, when three couples danced a minuet; but one girl "slipped and fell on her—ho, ho!"

In December 1948 Williams jotted in a notebook that he was in danger of over-working a certain vein in his writing: "loneliness, eroticism, repression, undefined spiritual longings: the intimate material of my own psyche is what I have filled my work with, and perhaps built it on, and now I have got to include, perhaps predominantly, some other things, and what are they?" It was not to be other "things" in *Dog Enchanted, The Rose Tattoo,* and some of Williams's plays that came after them, but a different tone, one of sardonic laughter—a laughter that recognizes the humor as well as the pain in our lives, recognizes that perfection and grace are but moments, followed by imperfection and clumsiness. Very much a part of the pain is that spiritual longing Williams mentioned, that perhaps can never be completely satisfied in our temporal existence. So part of the human condition is the loneliness often felt by Williams's characters, and by Williams himself.

That the rose imagery in *The Rose Tattoo* is a symbol of human love goes without saying, but it is worth noting for a moment the rose's association with spiritual love in Serafina's Catholic tradition. Mary is the Mystical Rose, the *Rosa sine spine* (Rose without thorns), and many of the cathedrals of Europe have a rose window dedicated to the Virgin. In the great hymn, *Salve Regina,* the faithful ask the Queen of Heaven to look upon humanity in its post-Edenic exile, its valley of tears, with eyes of mercy. Perhaps

Serafina's belief in the Holy Mother makes the world for her less cold, less lonely. Of her little shrine with the statue of the Madonna, Williams says in his Production Notes, "Our purpose is to show these gaudy, childlike mysteries with sentiment and humor in equal measure, without ridicule and with respect for the religious yearnings they symbolize." He attempted to assuage his own profound loneliness with companions for a night or, as with Merlo, a companion who shared his life for many years. "Desire is rooted in a longing for companionship," Williams noted in an interview, "a release from the loneliness that haunts every individual." That is what is at stake in *Dog Enchanted* and in *The Rose Tattoo*, and in so much of Williams's work. Paul tells Clara, "we are two lonely people," and when she thinks he has obeyed her request and gone, she "begins to weep very softly and forlornly." Alvaro tells Serafina, when she asks what he has to offer a woman, "Love and affection!—in a world that is lonely—and cold!" At the end of the play, the new life in her is not only the child she believes she has conceived, but her own self reborn like the phoenix. When she runs after love, and up the embankment toward Alvaro, Serafina's heart flies from the broken urn of ashes to become the *Rondinella felice*.

Jack Barbera
The University of Mississippi

# THE MEANING OF
# *THE ROSE TATTOO*

*The Rose Tattoo* is the Dionysian element in human life, its mystery, its beauty, its significance. It is that glittering quicksilver that still somehow manages to slip from under the down-pressed thumbs of the enormous man in the brass-buttoned uniform and his female partner with the *pince-nez* and the chalky smelling black skirts that make you sneeze as she brushes disdainfully past you. It is the dissatisfaction with empiric evidence that makes the poet and mystic, for it is the lyric as well as the Bacchantic impulse, and although the goat is one of its most immemorial symbols, it must not be confused with mere sexuality. The element is higher and more distilled than that. Its purest form is probably manifested by children and birds in their rhapsodic moments of flight and play, especially during the last few minutes of pale blue summer dusk before they light on branches and before their mothers call from the doors, *Come home!* It is not the obedient coming home and going to bed but it is the limitless world of the dream. It is the *rosa mystica,* the light on the bare golden flesh of a god whose back is turned to us or whose face is covered and who flies away from us when we call *Wait!* and rushes past us when we try to stop him. It is the fruit of the vine that takes earth, sun, and air and distills them into juices that deprive men not of reason but of a different thing called prudence. . . .

Finally and incidentally, it is the desire of an artist to work in new forms, however awkwardly at first, to break down barriers of what he has done before and what others have done better before and after and to crash, perhaps fatally, into some area that the bell-harness and rope would like to forbid him.

It may seem curious that I have chosen a woman to be the main protagonist of a play on such a theme. But in the blind and frenzied efforts of the widow, Serafina, to comprehend the mysteries of her dead husband, we sense and learn more about him than would have been possible through direct observation of the living man, the Dionysus himself. Dionysus, being mystery, is never seen clearly. He can not be confined to memory nor an urn, nor the conventions and proprieties of a plump little seamstress who wanted to fortify her happiness with the respect of the community. It was a mistake to fill the house with dummies. It took a long while to learn that eventually the faceless dummies must be knocked over, however elaborate their trappings. It took an almost literal unclothing, a public appearance in a wine-stained rayon slip, a fierce attack on a priest and the neighbor women, to learn that the blood of the wild young daughter was better, as a memorial, than ashes kept in a crematory urn.

In its treatment of this theme the play is no doubt more allusive than direct. Still more undoubtedly its theme overshadows the play. It is the homely light of a kitchen candle burned in praise of a god. I prefer a play to be not a noose but a net with fairly wide meshes. So many of its instants of revelation are wayward flashes, not part of the plan of an author but struck accidentally off, and perhaps these are closest to being a true celebration of the inebriate god.

1951

# A CHRONOLOGY

1907    June 3: Cornelius Coffin Williams and Edwina Estelle Dakin marry in Columbus, Mississippi.

1909    November 19: Sister, Rose Isabelle Williams, is born in Columbus, Mississippi.

1911    March 26: Thomas Lanier Williams III is born in Columbus, Mississippi.

1918    July: Williams family moves to St. Louis, Missouri.

1919    February 21: Brother, Walter Dakin Williams, is born in St. Louis, Missouri.

1928    Short story "The Vengeance of Nitocris" is published in *Weird Tales* magazine.

       July: Williams's grandfather, Walter Edwin Dakin (1857–1954), takes young Tom on a tour of Europe.

1929    September: Begins classes at the University of Missouri at Columbia.

1930    Writes the one-act play *Beauty is the Word* for a local contest.

1932    Summer: Fails ROTC and is taken out of college by his father and put to work as a clerk at the International Shoe Company.

1936    January: Enrolls in extension courses at Washington University, St. Louis.

1937    March 18 and 20: First full-length play, *Candles to the Sun*, is produced by the Mummers, a semi-professional theater company in St. Louis.

September: Transfers to the University of Iowa.

November 30 and December 4: *Fugitive Kind* is performed by the Mummers.

1938    Graduates from the University of Iowa with a degree in English.

Completes the play *Not About Nightingales*.

1939    *Story* magazine publishes "The Field of Blue Children" with the first printed use of his professional name, "Tennessee Williams."

Receives an award from the Group Theatre for a group of short plays collectively titled *American Blues*, which leads to his association with Audrey Wood, his agent for the next thirty-two years.

1940    January through June: Studies playwriting with John Gassner at the New School for Social Research in New York City.

December 30: *Battle of Angels*, starring Miriam Hopkins, suffers a disastrous first night during its out-of-town try-out in Boston and closes shortly thereafter.

1942    December: At a cocktail party thrown by Lincoln Kirstein in New York, meets James Laughlin, founder of New Directions, who is to become Williams' lifelong friend and publisher.

1943    January 13: A bilateral prefrontal lobotomy is performed on Rose Isabelle Williams, leaving her in a childlike mental state for the rest of her life.

Drafts a screenplay, *The Gentleman Caller*, while under contract in Hollywood with Metro Goldwyn Mayer: rejected by the studio, he later rewrites it as *The Glass Menagerie*.

October 13: A collaboration with his friend Donald Windham, *You Touched Me!* (based on a story by D. H. Lawrence), premieres at the Cleveland Playhouse.

1944    December 26: *The Glass Menagerie* opens in Chicago starring Laurette Taylor.

A group of poems titled "The Summer Belvedere" is published in *Five Young American Poets, 1944.* (All books listed here are published by New Directions unless otherwise indicated.)

1945    March 25: *Stairs to the Roof* premieres at the Pasadena Playhouse in California.

March 31: *The Glass Menagerie* opens on Broadway and goes on to win the Drama Critics Circle Award for best play of the year.

September 25: *You Touched Me!* opens on Broadway, and is later published by Samuel French.

December 27: *Wagons Full of Cotton and Other Plays* is published.

1947    Summer: Meets Frank Merlo (1929–1963) in Provincetown—starting in 1948 they become lovers and companions, and remain together for fourteen years.

December 3: *A Streetcar Named Desire,* directed by Elia Kazan and starring Jessica Tandy, Marlon Brando, Kim Hunter and Karl Malden, opens on Broadway to rave reviews and wins the Pulitzer Prize and the Drama Critics Circle Award.

1948    October 6: *Summer and Smoke* opens on Broadway and closes in just over three months.

1949    January: *One Arm and Other Stories* is published.

1950    The novel *The Roman Spring of Mrs. Stone* is published.

The film version of *The Glass Menagerie* is released.

1951    February 3: *The Rose Tattoo* opens on Broadway starring Maureen Stapleton and Eli Wallach and wins the Tony Award for best play of the year.

The film version of *A Streetcar Named Desire* is released starring Vivian Leigh as Blanche and Marlon Brando as Stanley.

1952    April 24: A revival of *Summer and Smoke* directed by José Quintero and starring Geraldine Page opens off-Broadway at the Circle at the Square and is a critical success.

The National Institute of Arts and Letters inducts Williams as a member.

1953    March 19: *Camino Real* opens on Broadway and after a harsh critical reception closes within two months.

1954    A book of stories, *Hard Candy*, is published in August.

1955    March 24: *Cat on a Hot Tin Roof* opens on Broadway directed by Elia Kazan and starring Barbara Bel Geddes, Ben Gazzara and Burl Ives. *Cat* wins the Pulitzer Prize and the Drama Critics Circle Award.

The film version of *The Rose Tattoo*, for which Anna Magnani later wins an Academy Award, is released.

1956    The film *Baby Doll*, with a screenplay by Williams and directed by Elia Kazan, is released amid some controversy and is blacklisted by Catholic leader Cardinal Spellman.

June: *In the Winter of Cities*, Williams's first book of poetry, is published.

1957    March 21: *Orpheus Descending*, a revised version of *Battle of Angels*, directed by Harold Clurman, opens on Broadway but closes after two months.

1958    February 7: *Suddenly Last Summer* and *Something Unspoken* open off-Broadway under the collective title *Garden District.*

The film version of *Cat on a Hot Tin Roof* is released.

1959    March 10: *Sweet Bird of Youth* opens on Broadway and runs for three months.

The film version of *Suddenly Last Summer*, with a screenplay by Gore Vidal, is released.

1960    November 10: The comedy *Period of Adjustment* opens on Broadway and runs for over four months.

The film version of *Orpheus Descending* is released under the title *The Fugitive Kind.*

1961    December 29: *The Night of the Iguana* opens on Broadway and runs for nearly ten months.

The film versions of *Summer and Smoke* and *The Roman Spring of Mrs. Stone* are released.

1962    The film versions of *Sweet Bird of Youth* and *Period of Adjustment* are released.

1963    January 15: *The Milk Train Doesn't Stop Here Anymore* opens on Broadway and closes immediately due to a blizzard and a newspaper strike. It is revived January 1, 1964, in a Broadway production starring Tallulah Bankhead and Tab Hunter and closes within a week.

September: Frank Merlo dies of lung cancer.

1964    The film version of *Night of the Iguana* is released.

1966    February 22: *Slapstick Tragedy* (*The Mutilated* and *The Gnädiges Fräulein*) runs on Broadway for less than a week.

December: A novella and stories are published under the title *The Knightly Quest.*

1968    March 27: *Kingdom of Earth* opens on Broadway under the title *The Seven Descents of Myrtle.*

The film version of *The Milk Train Doesn't Stop Here Anymore* is released under the title *Boom!*

1969    May 11: *In the Bar of a Tokyo Hotel* opens off-Broadway and runs for three weeks.

Committed by his brother Dakin for three months to the Renard Psychiatric Division of Barnes Hospital in St. Louis.

The film version of *Kingdom of Earth* is released under the title *The Last of the Mobile Hot Shots.*

Awarded Doctor of Humanities degree by the University of Missouri and a Gold Medal for Drama by the American Academy of Arts and Letters.

1970    February: A book of plays, *Dragon Country*, is published.

1971    Williams breaks with his agent Audrey Wood. Bill Barnes assumes his representation, and then later Mitch Douglas.

1972    April 2: *Small Craft Warnings* opens off-Broadway.

Williams is given a Doctor of Humanities degree by the University of Hartford.

1973    March 1: *Out Cry*, the revised version of *The Two-Character Play*, opens on Broadway.

1974    September: *Eight Mortal Ladies Possessed*, a book of short stories, is published.

Williams is presented with an Entertainment Hall of Fame Award and a Medal of Honor for Literature from the National Arts Club.

1975    The novel *Moise and the World of Reason* is published by Simon and Schuster and Williams's *Memoirs* is published by Doubleday.

1976    January 20: *This Is (An Entertainment)* opens in San Francisco at the American Conservatory Theater.

June: *The Red Devil Battery Sign* closes during its out-of-town tryout in Boston.

November 23: *Eccentricities of a Nightingale*, a rewritten version of *Summer and Smoke*, opens in New York.

April: Williams's second volume of poetry, *Androgyne, Mon Amour*, is published.

1977    May 11: *Vieux Carré* opens on Broadway and closes within two weeks.

1978    *Tiger Tail* premieres at the Alliance Theater in Atlanta, Georgia, and a revised version premieres the following year at the Hippodrome Theater in Gainsville, Florida.

1979    January 10: *A Lovely Sunday for Creve Coeur* opens off-Broadway.

*Kirche, Küche, Kinder* workshops off-Broadway at the Jean Cocteau Repertory Theater.

Williams is presented with a Lifetime Achievement Award at the Kennedy Center Honors in Washington by President Jimmy Carter.

1980    January 25: *Will Mr. Merriwether Return from Memphis?* premieres for a limited run at the Tennessee Williams Performing Arts Center in Key West, Florida.

March 26: Williams's last Broadway play, *Clothes for a Summer Hotel*, opens and closes after 15 performances.

1981    August 24: *Something Cloudy, Something Clear* premieres off-Broadway at the Jean Cocteau Repertory Theater.

1982    May 8: The second of two versions of *A House Not Meant to Stand* opens for a limited run at the Goodman Theater in Chicago.

1983     February 24: Williams is found dead in his room at the Hotel Elysee in New York City. Williams is later buried in St. Louis.

1984     July: *Stopped Rocking and Other Screenplays* is published.

1985     November: *Collected Stories*, with an introduction by Gore Vidal, is published.

1995     The first half of Lyle Leverich's important biography, *Tom: The Unknown Tennessee Williams*, is published by Crown Publishers.

1996     September 5: Rose Isabelle Williams dies in Tarrytown, New York.

         September 5: *The Notebook of Trigorin*, in a version revised by Williams, opens at the Cincinnati Playhouse in the Park.

1998     March 5: *Not About Nightingales* premieres at the Royal National Theatre in London, directed by Trevor Nunn, later moves to Houston, Texas, and opens November 25, 1999, on Broadway.

1999     November: *Spring Storm* is published.

2000     May: *Stairs to the Roof* is published.

         November: *The Selected Letters of Tennessee Williams, Volume I* is published.

2001     June: *Fugitive Kind* is published.

2002     April: *Collected Poems* is published.

2004     August: *Candles to the Sun* is published.

         November: *The Selected Letters of Tennessee Williams, Volume II* is published.

2005    April: *Mister Paradise and Other One-Act Plays* is published.

2008    April: *A House Not Meant to Stand* and *The Traveling Companion and Other Plays* are published.

        May 20: Walter Dakin Williams dies at the age of 89 in Belleville, Illinois.

# New Directions Paperbooks — a partial listing

Henry Miller, The Air-Conditioned Nightmare
  Big Sur & The Oranges of Hieronymus Bosch
  The Colossus of Maroussi
Yukio Mishima, Confessions of a Mask
  Death in Midsummer
Eugenio Montale, Selected Poems*
Vladimir Nabokov, Laughter in the Dark
  Nikolai Gogol
  The Real Life of Sebastian Knight
Pablo Neruda, The Captain's Verses*
  Love Poems*
  Residence on Earth*
Charles Olson, Selected Writings
George Oppen, New Collected Poems (with CD)
Wilfred Owen, Collected Poems
Michael Palmer, Thread
Nicanor Parra, Antipoems*
Boris Pasternak, Safe Conduct
Kenneth Patchen
  Memoirs of a Shy Pornographer
Octavio Paz, Selected Poems
  A Tale of Two Gardens
Victor Pelevin
  The Hall of the Singing Caryatids
  Omon Ra
Saint-John Perse, Selected Poems
Ezra Pound, The Cantos
  New Selected Poems and Translations
  Personae
Raymond Queneau, Exercises in Style
Qian Zhongshu, Fortress Besieged
Raja Rao, Kanthapura
Herbert Read, The Green Child
Kenneth Rexroth, Songs of Love, Moon & Wind
  Written on the Sky: Poems from the Japanese
Keith Ridgway, Hawthorn & Child
Rainer Maria Rilke
  Poems from the Book of Hours
Arthur Rimbaud, Illuminations*
  A Season in Hell and The Drunken Boat*
Guillermo Rosales, The Halfway House
Evelio Rosero, The Armies
  Good Offices
Joseph Roth, The Emperor's Tomb
Jerome Rothenberg, Triptych
Ihara Saikaku, The Life of an Amorous Woman
William Saroyan
  The Daring Young Man on the Flying Trapeze
Albertine Sarrazin, Astragal

Jean-Paul Sartre, Nausea
  The Wall
Delmore Schwartz
  In Dreams Begin Responsibilities
W. G. Sebald, The Emigrants
  The Rings of Saturn
  Vertigo
Aharon Shabtai, J'accuse
Hasan Shah, The Dancing Girl
C. H. Sisson, Selected Poems
Gary Snyder, Turtle Island
Muriel Spark, The Ballad of Peckham Rye
  A Far Cry From Kensington
  Memento Mori
George Steiner, My Unwritten Books
Antonio Tabucchi, Indian Nocturne
  Pereira Declares
Yoko Tawada, The Bridegroom Was a Dog
  The Naked Eye
Dylan Thomas, A Child's Christmas in Wales
  Collected Poems
  Under Milk Wood
Uwe Timm, The Invention of Curried Sausage
Charles Tomlinson, Selected Poems
Tomas Tranströmer
  The Great Enigma: New Collected Poems
Leonid Tsypkin, The Bridge over the Neroch
  Summer in Baden-Baden
Tu Fu, Selected Poems
Frederic Tuten, The Adventures of Mao
Paul Valéry, Selected Writings
Enrique Vila-Matas, Bartleby & Co.
  Dublinesque
Elio Vittorini, Conversations in Sicily
Rosmarie Waldrop, Driven to Abstraction
Robert Walser, The Assistant
  Microscripts
  The Tanners
Eliot Weinberger, An Elemental Thing
  Oranges and Peanuts for Sale
Nathanael West
  Miss Lonelyhearts & The Day of the Locust
Tennessee Williams, Cat on a Hot Tin Roof
  The Glass Menagerie
  A Streetcar Named Desire
William Carlos Williams, In the American Grain
  Selected Poems
  Spring and All
Louis Zukofsky, "A"
  Anew

*BILINGUAL EDITION

For a complete listing, request a free catalog from New Directions, 80 8th Avenue, NY NY 10011
or visit us online at www.ndpublishing.com